SWEET LAND, SWEET LIBERTY!

SWEET LAND, SWEET LIBERTY!

The story of America as found in the experiences of her people

A Rutledge Book
Prentice-Hall, Inc.
Englewood Cliffs, N.J

Based on the Alan Landsburg television series *The American Idea*

ISBN: 0-13-879247-X
Library of Congress Catalog Card Number: 74-76862
Copyright 1974 in all countries of the International
    Copyright Union by Alan Landsburg Productions, Inc.
    All rights reserved including the right of reproduction
    in whole or in part.
Prepared and produced by The Ridge Press, Inc.—
    Rutledge Books Division, 25 West 43rd Street,
    New York, N.Y. 10036
Book Project Editor: Mercer Field
All illustrations from Alan Landsburg Productions
Published in 1974 by Prentice-Hall, Inc., Englewood
    Cliffs, N.J.
Printed in Italy by Mondadori, Verona

Beginnings 9

The South 47

Going West 71

The Indian 115

The Cowboy 135

The Immigrant 159

Rediscovery 199

America—How They Saw It 209

WE TELL our freedom backward by the land. We tell our past by the gravestones and the apple trees. But the story of America is also to be found in the experiences of her people. For in truth they've chronicled their own history —and more than with gravestones and apple trees. They've left letters and diaries, family albums and recollections, poems, almanacs, and town records. And through them a special history of the country unfolds, the human story of what we are, what we hope to be, as a people, as a place, and as an idea.

That is what we, as television producers, set out to do: to express this American idea as hour-long broadcasts, made possible by the Ford Motor Company. Now, in these book pages, the publishers have drawn their text from our thousands of hours of research, and their illustrations from our reservoir of color photography taken by cameramen who roamed America on land and airborne in helicopters, to tell on the printed page this American idea.

The quoted words you will find here were first spoken or recorded in diaries or

almanacs or journals, and richly relate how it was that America began, grew, and became what she is. The additional material, in italics, is from the original television soundtrack and includes the voices of actors from that production, Ossie Davis and Kirk Douglas.

Michel Guillaume Jean de Crévecoeur, in his *Letters from an American Farmer,* in 1782, wrote: "Here, in America, individuals of all nations are melted into a new race of men."

Thomas Jefferson observed: "Those who cultivate the earth are the most vigorous, the most independent, the most valuable citizens. They are tied to their country and wedded to its liberty by the most lasting bonds." He also said: "My God! how little do my countrymen know what precious blessings they are in possession of, and which no other people on earth enjoy!"

Or, as a later American said: "God must have meant this land to be the last one found because it's sure his most beautiful work."

Alan Landsburg

Beginnings

From sea it stretches to shining sea, the world's most diverse landscape, a place called America.

No single chronicle tells her story, but soar as an eagle across her lands and you will sense her strength. Listen to her people, past and present, and you will feel the roots of her greatness.

Opposite: *The Massachusetts shore in winter*

Being thus past the vast ocean
and sea of troubles before in
their preparation, they had
now no friends to welcome
them nor Inns to entertain and
refresh their weatherbeaten

bodies. No houses, nor much
less towns to repair to, to seek
for succor. But they smelled
the trees of the new land and
rejoiced.

Diary of William Bradford
on board the *Mayflower* (1630)

THE REASONS for the great Puritan
migration were primarily religious.
These people felt that they did not
have the opportunity to create what they
called the City of God in England. The
world of James I and Charles I of
England was, as they saw it, licentious and
loose and . . . bad. They wanted to come to
a new country which they would make in
what they believed to be God's image. It
was rather a strict idea, but they had a
very strong belief that they could
communicate directly to God through
the Bible.

The second reason they came was that
they saw a great opportunity to have land.
Land was scarce in England, and it
belonged to the wealthy. The Puritans
were almost all tenants, but in the new
land they could become freeholders, which
was the great ambition of almost all
Europeans, particularly English people.
They wished to have land and so they

came to the new country . . . and they
farmed it and they made their own
homesteads. You can see this through the
whole of American history—the gradual
extension of the frontier, the desire for
freedom, for independence, obtainable
by open land.

The really important gift of the Puritans
to this country is the idea of questioning.
Doubt yourself, doubt what others tell
you, and then perhaps you will be lucky
enough to find the right way.

Thomas B. Adams
Lincoln, Massachusetts
January, 1973

Boston harbor in the late eighteenth century

The month of June, 1622, it was my chance to arrive in the parts of New England. And when I had more seriously considered of the beauty of the place, I didn't think in all the known world that it could be paralleled. If this land be not rich, then is the whole world poor.

William Bradford, *History of Plimmoth Plantation* (1630)

The Mayflower Compact acknowledged the fear and summarized the hope.

Governor William Bradford described the expectations of the Pilgrims to these shores: "The place they had thoughts of was one of those vast and unemployed countries of America, which are fruitful and fit for habitation, being devoid of all civil inhabitants, where there are only savage and brutish men."

They found instead a difficult land and gentle native Indians. Massasoit, Chief of the Wampanoags, freely granted to Pilgrim leader Edward Winslow all the land the immigrants would need.

The Mayflower brought the Pilgrims. Half its complement were tradesmen. Tension stretched between the groups. Both sides, foreseeing the need for order, drew up "a covenant to combine ourselves together in a civil body politick for our better ordering, preservation and furtherance of the ends."

The first farmers came to Peacham, Vermont, under a grant allowing them to own their land if, according to the charter, they would plant five acres in five years. According to King's Law, trees of more than twenty-three inches in diameter were reserved for the main masts of his majesty's ships. And so the floor boards of Peacham's early homes were twenty-two inches in width.

THE GROUND here produces Indian corn, and all kinds of English grain to perfection, likewise all garden vegetables in great plenty, and they have very promising orchards of excellent fruit. Many things grow here in the open fields which the climate of Scotland will not produce, such as melons, cucumbers, pumpkins, and the like. . . . Sugar can be made here in abundance in March and April from the maple tree which grows in great plenty. In short, no place which we have seen is better furnished with food and the necessaries of life, and even some of its luxuries, or where the people live more comfortable than here. . . . Clearing land seems to be no hardship as it is commonly done from five to six dollars per acre.

James Whitlaw describing Newbury, Vt., in *Peacham*, Ernest L. Bogart (Montpelier, Vt., 1948)

Above and below: *Villages in Vermont, early 1800s*

CHEAP LAND was what first brought people to Peacham. Of course, you know it was all wooded at that time. The land was something like three pence an acre, and that is why the Scots settled there. They looked far and wide, even going down into North Carolina, looking for land. Peacham reminded them of Scotland, and it wasn't far from the Connecticut River. The rivers were used a lot in those days since there were no roads. Most of the settlers, a good many of them, came from Connecticut and Massachusetts. In fact, for a while Vermont was called New Connecticut.

In 1797 this country was beginning to be developed to the point where they needed a courthouse and an institution of higher learning, because there were only the one-room schools which gave elementary education only. Peacham had a choice of having the County Seat or the Academy, and it decided for the Academy. The County Seat went to Danville.

I've never seen anyone yet who was born or lived in Vermont but who cherished the idea of returning. Because you can't find this kind of life in many places. It's getting more noticeable as time goes on.

Town Clerk
Peacham, Vermont
May, 1972

IN MAY 1775 my Farther, my self in my 14th year, with 2 hired men, set out for Peacham, no road, nothing but a spotted line with know and then a bush, cut 20 miles from the settlement in Newbury. my farther led his horse loded with Provisions. We drove a yoak of oxen and a cow (that was expected to calve within the month) and when we got on to the ground we found on the lot adjoining the one my Farther had pitched, Robert Cour [Carr] in a small camp, whair we pitched till we bilt a log house and bound it with bark.

"thair was Dr. John Skeels, Coll. Frey Bailey, John Sanborn, and some others that come on that spring, and a number more through the sumer. That sumer my Farther clared of a number of acres & sewed six or 8 acres with winter wheat, and he hyered 10 acres, to be clared of [off] for to be sewad with oats the nest year.

In the fall we all retreated to Haverhill, N. H. the next spring, in March, 1776, part of Butler's Rigmen was going through the woods to St. Johns, on their way through Peacham, my Farther thought it a good time to go on with the first company to Peacham and prepare for making shugar, and I with him. he took

his old pung with his Provisions &
Blankets & Snowshoes. started with the
first Company.

The year before, several Scotch
Famerlys had got on to Ryegate . . . and
they had kept a sled road as far as their,
and the Solders had slays to carry thair
packs as far as thair. my Farther had a
boy that cam with us, to take his horse
back. he gave me for a pack 3 pecks of
meal, my Blanket & Snowshoes. he took his
pack, and went on with the Pitch in frunt.
my Pack was so havy I was not able to
keep up with him, and had to linger
behind among the Solders. . .

The next day my Farther & my self
Came to our house, which was a mile from
whare the track that the Solders past
to the west of us. my Farther and my self
went emeadately about making troughs
for sugring, and in 8 or ten days we had
got prepared for taping our trees. my
Farther got 1 or 2 kittles halled from
Ryegate on hand sleds, and he went home
to Haverhill and left me, for a few days
to take care of the sap. wc made
consedrable shuger, and after the snow
went of several people returned to their
farmes as they called them.

Diary of Jonathan Elkins, Jr. (1777),
in *Peacham*, Ernest L. Bogart
(Montpelier, Vt., 1948)

Although we were an outpost and had but six or eight men in town, we sent two of them–James Bailey and Moses Chamberlain–for we feared if the British were not going to be stopped, we shall all be ruined.

Private John Skeels left Peacham to fight in the Revolutionary War with his required equipment–one musket, one bullet pouch, and one tomahawk.

Reminiscences of Jonathan Elkins, in *Peacham*, Ernest L. Bogart (Montpelier, Vt., 1948)

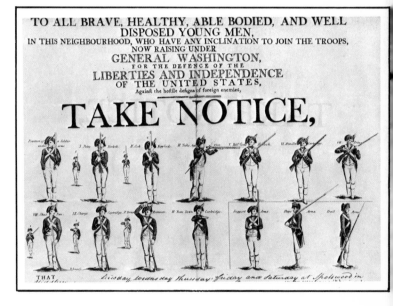

Fill your cellar, and fill your larder, for then you can go into the siege of winter with a zest, go to the cellar stairs, look at the preparations, smell the apples. . . . It is a milk and sugar country. I get what runs from the trees and the cows.

Robert Frost

With freedom Peacham would be governed by the town meeting, of which Emerson wrote: "The poor and the rich gave counsel. It was a free strife and an assurance of man's capacity for self-government."

It was another part of the American dream that took root here. It has to do with clear and simple values, with hard work and respect for each other and the land. These are stated in the rich accents of her people.

Farming is a good life. You get something to eat every day from the animals and the gardens or from your fields, or even from the woods; if you get hard up, you have to sell your cattle for something, you can go out and hunt awhile. It's far from getting rich from farming—it's almost impossible. When the time comes to sell out, well then you have a pocket full of money. That's the only time. Of course, it is nice to have a pocket full of cash when you're traveling

around and like to see different
things, but then if you look close
enough, you can see plenty right
here.

Charles A. Choate
Peacham, Vermont
May, 1972

I can't get religion inside any
concrete structure. I get it
when the sun comes up on the
fields, when the dew is like
pearls.

Hugh Tuttle
New England farmer

Opposite: *Pastureland in the Green Mountains, Vermont*

Below: *A Vermont covered bridge in the spring*

Above and below: *Livestock on a Vermont farm*

Above and below: *General stores in Vermont*

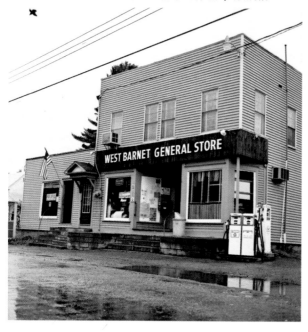

Right: *Fishing boats in a Massachusetts harbor*
Following pages: *Ice on the shore of a Cape Cod fishing village*

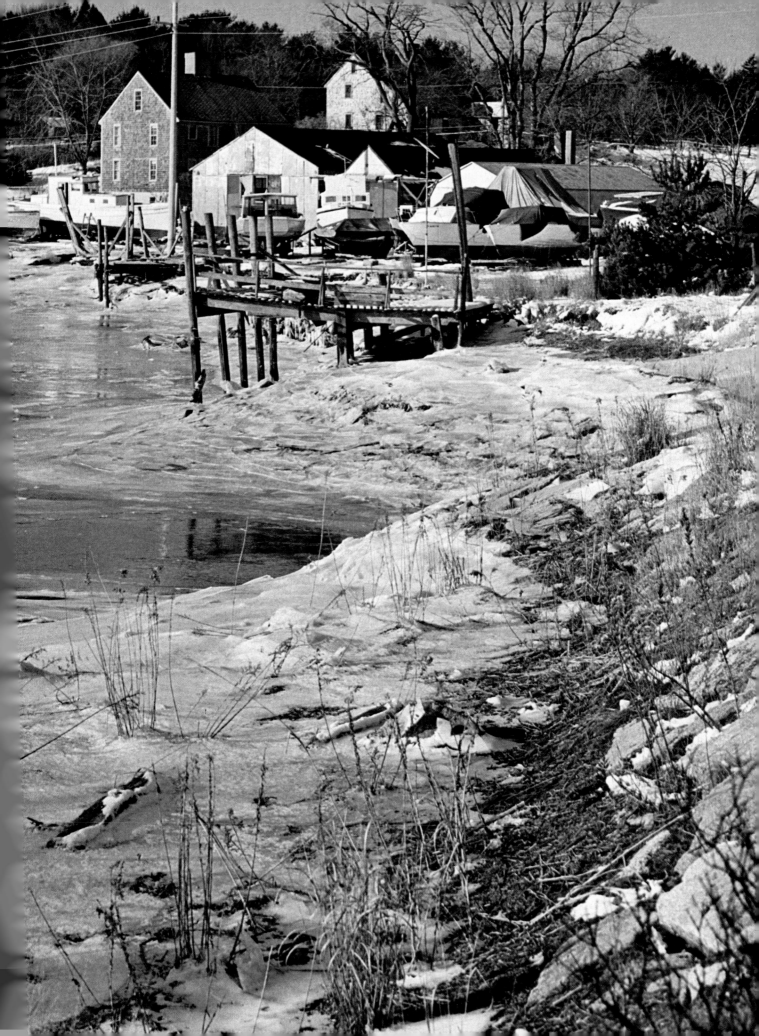

All persons living in this
province . . . that hold
themselves obliged . . . to live
peaceably and justly in civil
society shall in no ways be
molested or prejudiced for
their religious persuasion
or practice.

William Penn

Opposite: *Newly plowed farmland in Pennsylvania*

MANY PERSONS in Europe having by letters expressed to the writer of this, who is well acquainted with North America, their desire of transporting and establishing themselves in that country, but who appear to have formed through ignorance, mistaken ideas and expectations of what is to be obtained here, he thinks it may be useful . . . if he gives some clearer and truer notions of that part of the world than appear to have hitherto prevailed. . . .

The truth is that though there are in that country few people so miserable as the poor of Europe, there are also very few that in Europe would be called rich . . . most people cultivate their own lands, or follow some handicraft or merchandise. . . . It is true that letters and mathematical knowledge are in esteem there, but they are at the same time more common than is apprehended; there being already existing nine colleges or universities: viz., four in New England, and one in each of the provinces of New York, New Jersey, Pennsylvania, Maryland, and Virginia, all furnished with learned professors; besides a number of smaller academies. . . . Of civil officers . . . there are few . . . and it is a rule established in some of the states that no office should be so profitable as to make it desirable. . . . The Constitution of Pennsylvania runs expressly in these words: "As every freeman, to preserve his independence (if he has not a sufficient estate), ought to have some profession, calling, trade, or farm, whereby he may honestly subsist, there can be no necessity for, nor use in, establishing offices of profit, the usual effects of which are dependence and servility unbecoming freemen, in the possessors and expectants; faction, contention, corruption, and disorder among the people. Wherefore, whenever an office through increase of fees or otherwise, becomes so profitable as to occasion many to apply for it, the profits ought to be lessened by the legislature."

. . . It cannot be worth any man's while, who has a means of living at home, to expatriate himself in hopes of obtaining a profitable civil office in America. . . . Much less it is advisable for a person to go thither who has no other quality to recommend him but his birth. In Europe it has indeed its value; but it is a commodity that cannot be carried to a

worse market than that of America, where people do not inquire concerning a stranger: *What is he?* but: *What can he do?* . . . Strangers are welcome, because there is room enough for them all, but therefore the old inhabitants are not jealous of them; the laws protect them sufficiently so that they have no need of the patronage of great men. . . . One or two years' residence gives him all the rights of a citizen; but the government does not, at present, whatever it may have done in former times, hire people to become settlers, by paying their passages. . . . In short, America is the land of labor.

Benjamin Franklin,
Information to Those Who Would Remove to America (1782)

Amish, Quaker, Pilgrim, and Puritan, they came and millions followed. The miracle is not that they merged into a single nation but that they found a place to exist side by side, linked by the fragile concept of states united in a quest for freedom that existed nowhere else in the world.

WE DO NOT care for fellowship with any churches that allow or uphold any unfruitful works such as worldliness, fashionable attire, bed courtship, habitual smoking or drinking, non-assurance of salvation or anything contrary to sound doctrine.

Amish Articles of Faith (1633)

THE PEOPLE are a Collection of divers Nations in Europe: As, French, Dutch, Germans, Sweeds, Danes, Finns, Scotch, Irish and English; and of the last equal to all the rest: And, which is admirable, not a Reflection on that Account: But as they are of one kind, and in one Place and under One Allegiance, so they live like People of One Country, which Civil Union has had a considerable influence towards the prosperity of that place.

Philadelphia . . . is two Miles long, and a Mile broad, and at each end it lies that mile upon a Navigable River. The scituation high and dry, yet replenished with running streams. Besides the High Street, that runs in the middle from River to River, and is an hundred foot broad, it has Eight streets more that run the same course . . . And besides Broad Street, which crosseth the Town in the middle, and is also an hundred foot wide, there are twenty streets more, that run the same course . . . The names of those Streets are mostly taken from the things that Spontaneously grow in the Country, As Vine Street, Mulberry Street, Chestnut Street, Wallnut Street, Strawberry Street, Cranberry Street, Plumb Street, Hickery Street, Pine Street, Oake Street, Beach Street, Ash Street, Popler Street, Sassafrax Street, and the like.

. . . The Town advanced to Three hundred and fifty-seven Houses; divers of them large, well built, with good Cellars, three stories, and some with Balconies. . . .

There inhabits most sorts of useful Tradesmen, As Carpenters, Joyners, Bricklayers, Masons, Plasterers, Plumers, Smiths, Glasiers, Taylers, Shoemakers, Butchers, Bakers, Brewers, Glovers, Tanners, Felmongers, Wheelrights, Millrights, Shiprights, Boatrights, Ropemakers, Saylmakers, Blockmakers, Turners, etc.

William Penn,
A Further Account of the Province of Pennsylvania (1685)

Life in Philadelphia, ca. 1800: An oyster seller at night (facing page) ; *a stagecoach* (top left) *and the market* (bottom left) *on High Street; going to meeting Sunday morning* (above)

ONE OF my "Dutch" neighbors, who, from a shoemaker, became the owner of two farms, said to me, "The woman is more than half"; and his own very laborious wife . . . had indeed been so.

The woman (in common speech, "the old woman") milks, raises the poultry, has charge of the garden—sometimes digging the ground herself, and planting and hoeing, with the assistance of her daughters and the "maid," when she has one. . . . She has a quantity of cabbages and of "red beets," of onions and of early potatoes, in her garden, a plenty of cucumbers for winter pickles, and store of string-beans and tomatoes, with some sweet potatoes. . . .

In winter mornings perhaps the farmer's wife goes out to milk in the stable with a lantern, while her daughters get breakfast; has her house "redd up" about eight o'clock, and is prepared for several hours' sewing before dinner, laying by great piles of shirts for summer. . . . At the spring cleaning the labors of the women folk are increased by whitewashing the picket-fences.

Great are the household labors in harvest; but the cooking and baking in the hot weather are cheerfully done for the men, who are toiling in hot suns and stifling barns. Four meals are common at this season. . . . I heard of one "Dutch" girl's making some fifty pies a week in harvest; for if you have four meals a day, and pie at each, many are required. We have great faith in pie. . . . Friday is baking-day. The "Dutch" housewife is very fond of baking in the brick oven, but the scarcity of wood must gradually accustom us to the great cooking-stove. . . .

The majority keep one fire in winter. This is in the kitchen. . . . An adjoining room or building is the wash-house, where butchering, soap-making, etc., are done by the help of a great kettle hung in the fireplace, not set in brickwork. . . . These arrangements are not very favorable to bathing in cold weather; indeed, to wash the whole person is not very common, in summer or in winter.

Phoebe Earle Gibbons,
Pennsylvania Dutch and Other Essays (1882)

The York Hotels, Kept In 1800.

No Better. And good Cooks Can be found no where to prepare victuals for the table, As these Taverns. See the names—Mrs. Abraham Miller, mrs. Polly waltemyer. mrs. Goster, mrs. Laub, mrs. Upp. mrs. Rumel, mrs. baltzers Spangler. mrs. George Hay, mrs. Beard. and mrs. Eichelberger. not far from town, the two last names. old Style Cooking.

the Bake oven, bakin Bread.

Smokeing Sau and Sall

the had plenty of raw Materials, to Cook them, Beef. veal. Lam, Mutton. Pork. and fish. oysters, Poultry. Eggs. Butter, Cheese. milk and honey. And all Kind of vegetables—and fruit. See mrs. Hersh in 1809. She Could take every—bone out of A Chicken, for the table it was good to Carve. for the Customers at her Tavern.

After—frying the Sausage— the potatos put in the pan.

Little Sally.

mrs. Lottman frying Sweetpotatos and give to Lewis Miller, Some of them the first I ever tasted the where good Eating. It was in her tavern. South George Street. 1799.

THE TRAVELLING on these roads [in western Pennsylvania] in every direction is truly astonishing, even at this inclement season, but in the spring and fall, I am informed that it is beyond all conception. . . . The travellers are wagonners, carrying produce to, and bringing back foreign goods from the different shipping ports on the shores of the Atlantick, particularly Philadelphia and Baltimore:—Packers with from one to twenty horses . . . Countrymen . . . carrying salt . . . for the curing of their beef, pork, venison, &c.,—Families removing farther back into the country, some with cows, oxen, horses, sheep, and hogs, and all their farming implements and domestick utensils, and some without; some with wagons, some with carts and some on foot, according to the abilities:— The residue, who make use of the best accommodations on the roads, are country merchants, judges and lawyers attending the courts, members of the legislature, and the better class of settlers removing back. All the first four descriptions carry provisions for themselves and horses, live most miserably, and wrapped in blankets, occupy the floor of the bar rooms of the taverns where they stop each night, which the landlords give them the use of, with as much wood as they choose to burn, in consideration of the money they pay them for whiskey, of which they drink great quantities. . . . The latter description of travellers travel as in other countries— making use of and paying for their regular meals, beds, &c.

Fortescue Cuming,
*Sketches of a Tour to the Western Country,
Year 1839*

We arrived at this place [Schenectady, New York] at half past ten. From the cars we proceeded to enter our names for the Packet Boat.... These Boats have *three* horses, go at a quicker rate, and have the preference in going through the locks, carry no freight, are built extremely light, and have quite Genteel Men for their Captains, and use *silver* plate. The distance between Schenectady and Utica is eighty Miles, the passage is $3.50, which includes board....

The Bridges on the Canal are very low, particularly the old ones. Indeed they are so low as to scarcely allow the baggage to clear.... Every Bridge makes us bend double if seated on anything, and in many cases you have to lie on your back. The Man at the helm gives the word to the passengers: "Bridge," "very low Bridge," "the lowest in the Canal," as the case may be.

New York to Niagara, 1836:
The Journal of Thomas S. Woodcock,
ed. Deoch Fulton (New York, 1938)

THE EARTH, by God's blessing, has more than answered our expectation; the poorest places in our Judgment producing large Crops of Garden Stuff and Grain. . . .

Upon Tryal we find that the Corn and Roots that grow in England thrive very well there, as Wheat, Barly, Rye, Oats, Buck-Wheat, Pease, Beans, Cabbages, Turnips, Carrets, Parsnups, Colleflowers, Asparagus, Onions, Charlots, Garlick and Irish Potatos; we have also the Spanish and very good Rice, which do not grow here. . . .

The Weeds of our Woods feed our Cattle to the Market as well as Dary. I have seen fat Bullocks brought thence to Market before Mid Summer. Our Swamps or Marshes yeeld us course Hay for the Winter.

English Grass Seed takes well, which will give us fatting Hay in time. Of this I made an Experiment in my own Court Yard, upon sand that was dug out of my Cellar, with seed that had lain in a Cask open to the weather two Winters and a Summer; I caus'd it to be sown in the beginning of the month called April, and a fortnight before Midsummer it was fit to Mow. . . .

Mighty Whales roll upon the Coast, near the Mouth of the Bay of Delaware. Eleven caught and workt into Oyl one Season. We justly hope a considerable profit by a Whalery; they being so numerous and the Shore so suitable.

Sturgeon play continually in our Rivers in Summer; And though the way of cureing them be not generally known, yet by a Receipt I had of one Collins . . . I did so well preserve some, that I had them good there three months of the Summer . . .

. . . Shads are excellent Fish and of the Bigness of our largest Carp: They are so Plentiful, that Captain Smyth's Overseer at the Skulkil, drew 600 and odd at one Draught; 300 is no wonder; 100 familiarly. . . . the Herring . . . swarm in such shoales that it is hardly Credible; in little Creeks, they almost shovel them up in their tubs. There is the Catfish, or Flathead, Lampry, Eale, Trout, Perch, black and white, Smelt, Sunfish, etc.; also Oysters, Cockles, Cunks, Crabs, Mussles, Mannanoses. . . .

. . . Beef is commonly sold at the rate of two pence per Pound; and Pork for two pence half penny; Veal and Mutton at three pence or three pence half penny, that Country mony; an English Shilling going for fifteen pence. Grain sells by the Bushel; Wheat at four shillings; Rye, and excellent good, at three shillings . . . Indian Corn, two shillings six pence . . .

There is so great an encrease of Grain by the dilligent application of People to Husbandry that, within three Years, some Plantations have got Twenty Acres in Corn, some Forty, some Fifty.

William Penn,
A Further Account of the Province of Pennsylvania (1685)

The South

To relieve the wants of poor people, and to protect his Majesty's subjects in South Carolina, a colony should be settled . . . on the southern frontiers of Carolina.

Royal charter granted to Savannah (1732)

Savannah, Georgia, was founded as a colony for the poor. James Oglethorpe's domain was to be a buffer zone between Spanish Florida and the prospering plantations of Carolina. The first settlers of Savannah were considered expendables.

ONE HUNDRED and thirty-five years ago a small tribe of Indians occupied the bluff upon which the city of Savannah now stands. Then the Indian's canoe, only, ruffled the placid waters of the Savannah; now steam and sail vessels from every clime, attracted by the fruits of Savannah's commerce, plough its bosom, coming and going, with keels deeply sunk in the water. Then the smoke curled lazily upward from a few wigwams; now fiery furnaces belch forth volumes of ruddy flame, and on every hand is heard the din of hammers and bellows, the voices of men echoing from the manufactories, wharves, and places of business, where a numerous population are plying the tireless fingers of industry in the creation of substantial wealth. Then the woods resounded with the savage warwhoop; now the no less discordant, but more civilized, steam whistle is heard as the heavily laden trains pass to and fro on the iron arms which have been stretched in every direction, clasping in their embrace some of the choicest regions of the country. On every hand are elegant and luxurious mansions, gardens teeming with flowers of richest and rarest hue; churches and humane institutions; colleges and schools; squares and parks thronged with mature and youthful beauty, making the balmy atmosphere vocal with sounds of human life and joy—all attesting wealth, refinement, piety, benevolence, intelligence, health, and happiness.

By the seventh of July [1733], one hundred and fifty more settlers arrived, a large number of whom came at their own expense; a large tract of land was cleared and a number of houses erected, and it was resolved to designate the town, wards, squares, and streets with formal ceremonies. . . . Four days after these ceremonies a colony of Israelites arrived direct from London. . . . Some persons in England became offended when the arrival of this party was reported, and wrote to the Trustees, stating that they would not contribute money for the support of the colony so long as the Hebrews remained. The Trustees wrote to the commissioners who had sent them over. . . . Oglethorpe was also written to by the Trustees. . . . In reply, Oglethorpe praised their good conduct, and especially commended the skill and kindness of Dr. Nunis, who, since his arrival, had rendered valuable services to the sick colonists. Oglethorpe very wisely refused to move them, and time has proven that, had he complied with the request of the Trustees, the colony would have lost some of its most moral and industrious citizens. . . . About this period the alligators, which had at first been frightened away by the bustle and noise made in building houses, felling trees, and the like, grew bold, and amused themselves by strolling about town at night, much to the annoyance and terror of the inhabitants.

F. D. Lee and J. L. Agnew,
Historical Record of the City of Savannah (1869)

48

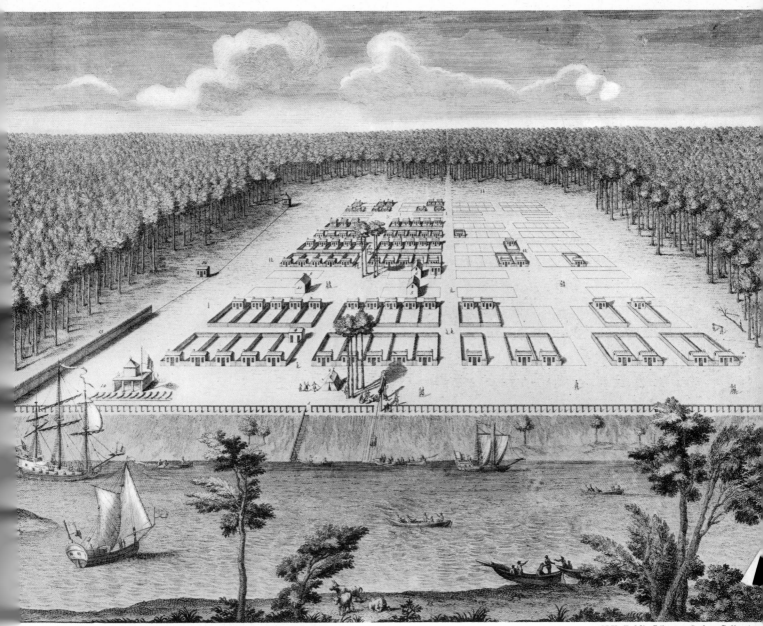

Savannah, Georgia, in 1734, one year after it was founded

Those who have held onto or adopted what remains of Savannah's plantation life cling to something more than history. From the very beginning, it meant home and the lasting value of family and belonging to the land, for the land was a means to a way of life. In a diary for her children many years ago, Mary Lane, who with her husband owned Lebanon Plantation, may have said it best:

"We have planted oranges and sold them. Planted cabbages, potatoes, corn, and cotton. I imagine the ledger is still in the red. But what does it matter, when to us all remain the everlasting memories of a family united by bonds of long days and nights together."

To most of us, they seem part of a distant and remote past, part of a story on the land that ended more than a hundred years ago. And yet there are families here descended in direct line from those English settlers who journeyed to Georgia with James Oglethorpe in 1733. Some of them still hold the same land that was granted to their families by George II.

Early immigrants to the South developed a character and style that lingers even today. They adopted a life similar to that of country manors in England. The French aristocrat Alexis de Tocqueville noted: "Everything was grave, serious, and solemn in the North. It seemed to be the domain of intelligence, as the South was that of sensual delight."

Life in the early days was something less than a picnic, especially for the women. They had somehow to make a home on the plantation. According to the family records at Wormsloe, in Georgia, much of the responsibility fell to a young teen-age daughter, Mary Jones.

With her mother ill and her father and brothers absent on military expeditions, young Mary had to run the plantation and tend the silkworms, Wormsloe's first business. It also fell to her to command the fort there during their absence. According to the family history, she successfully defended it on at least one occasion against attacks by Indians, holding them off by musket fire through a window. But there are enough reminders of her limited status as a woman. Oglethorpe's Rules stipulated that the land should all be held "entail male." This meant that inheritance passed only to men. Ironically, women could have no franchise because, it was said, landholders had to be able to defend their property. There were other rules too—part of Oglethorpe's Utopian dream for Georgia. There was to be no rum and brandy, and no slaves.

NO SLAVES. That is, until they changed the rules. In 1750 the new law was passed under pressure from the landholders, who were threatening to move across the river into South Carolina where a planter could own slaves—where you could see the prosperity. So the American idea, that a man could own land, had its exceptions. I was born in Georgia, about 106 miles from Savannah. My ancestors were slaves there, lived in a cabin, the shutters painted blue for good luck. As a boy, I heard the stories of the slave life on the plantation. Our conditions may have varied from owner to owner, place to place. Most of it followed from the Rules. A slave code of Georgia, dated 1755, stated:

"All negroes who are now or shall hereafter be on this province and all their issue and offspring born or to be born will be and are declared to be and remain hereafter absolute slaves and shall follow the condition of the mother, and shall be deemed in law to be chattels personal in the hands of their owners and possessors. For anyone trying to teach a slave to read or write, there is a fine of fifteen pounds English. For working them more than sixteen hours a day, the fine is three. Slaves cannot leave the plantation without a ticket signed by their masters." If they were found without that ticket, then they could receive "up to twenty lashes with a whip. No more than seven slaves may travel together on the high roads unless accompanied by a white person." The reason: to prevent them from congregating. And every plantation developed an elaborate patrol system to keep slaves under surveillance. "Run, run, the pat-a-rol will get you." That's the way the old slave song goes.

Ossie Davis

Black sharecropper on the porch of his cabin, with cotton and yams, Arkansas, 1935

My grandfather took over
Belleview and operated
it as a cotton plantation,
experimenting in all sorts of
agriculture. He grew rice
in the swamps, but
unsuccessfully. Today you
can still see where the canals
were dug for the rice fields.
He also tried to grow tobacco,
but the land just wasn't the
type, so he concentrated
on cotton.

My grandfather and a
friend of his owned a store
together, and when they
decided to break up the
partnership, they couldn't
decide on who would get
young Tom Hughes, the
foreman. So they shot craps
for him and my grandfather
won. Tom stayed with my
family until his death, when
he was in his nineties.

Porter Carswell
Belleview Plantation, Waynesboro, Georgia
August, 1972

Cotton pickers ready for work at 6:30 A.M., Arkansas, 1935

Photo by Ben Shahn; N.Y. Public Library, Picture Collection

In Arkansas, 1935, an Ozark mountain family (opposite) *and a sharecropper mother and child* (above)

I T IS the common supposition that our southern mountain women . . . are . . . spiritlessly submissive. And it is true that from time beyond question, it has been "manners" for the mountain woman to obey, just as it is a deep-seated matter of fact that the mountain man is lord and master. . . . As one . . . West Virginia male put it comfortably, "Thar's only two places for a woman: one's in the kitchen, and t'other's in the feather bed."

He forgot their outdoor chores. All mountain women take pleasure in their flowers and their gardens. But when gathering fodder, helping plow, splitting kindling, taking her end of the crosscut saw, and dynamiting stumps are added to her natural pleasure in planting and watching things grow, it is apt to get "a least mite wearisome."

Alberta Pierson Hannum, "The Mountain People," in *The Great Smokies and the Blue Ridge* (ed. Roderick Peattie) (New York, 1943)

New Orleans, January 12th, 1819

EVERYTHING had an odd look. For 25 years I have been a traveler only between New York and Richmond, and I confess that I felt myself in some degree again a Cockney, for it was impossible not to stare at a sight wholly new even to one who has traveled much in Europe and America. . . .

Along the levee . . . were ranged two rows of market people, some having stalls or tables with a tilt or awning of canvas, but the majority having their wares lying on the ground, perhaps on a piece of canvass, or a parcel of palmetto leaves. The articles to be sold were not more various than the sellers. White men and women, and of all hues of brown, and of all classes of face, from round Yankees, to grisly, lean Spaniards, black negroes and negresses, filthy Indians half naked, mullattoes, curly- and straight-haired, quateroons of all shades, long-haired and frizzled, the women dressed in the most flaming yellow and scarlet gowns, the men capped and hatted. Their wares consisted of as many kinds as their faces: innumerable wild ducks, oysters, poultry of all kinds, fish, bananas, piles of oranges, sugar cane, sweet and Irish potatoes, corn in the ear and husked, apples, carrots, and all sorts of other roots, eggs, trinkets, tin ware, dry goods—in fact of more and odder things to be sold in that manner and place than I can enumerate. . . .

What is the state of society in New Orleans? The Americans, coming hither to make money and considering their residence as temporary, are doubly active in availing themselves of the enlarged opportunities of becoming wealthy which the place offers. . . . Their business is to make money. They are in an eternal bustle.

Benjamin Latrobe,
Impressions Respecting New Orleans

Opposite and below: *On the levee, New Orleans Louisiana*

WE ARRIVED at the commencement of a cane country, traveled about thirty miles through thick cane and reed, and as the cane ceased, we began to discover the pleasing and rapturous appearance of the plains of Kentucky. A new sky and strange earth seemed to be presented to our view. So rich a soil we had never seen before, covered with clover in full bloom; the woods were abounding with wild game—turkeys so numerous that it might be said they appeared but one flock, universally scattered in the woods. . . . We felt ourselves as passengers through a wilderness. . . .

On the 25th March, 1775, we were fired on by the Indians, in our camp asleep, about an hour before day. . . . So fatal and tragical an event cast a deep gloom of melancholy over all our prospects . . . hope vanished from the most of us, and left us suspended in the tumult of uncertainty and conjecture. Colonel Boon, and a few others, appeared to possess firmness and fortitude. . . . My situation was critical and dangerous, being then a youth, three hundred miles from white inhabitants. . . . My wounds, pronounced by some to be mortal, produced very serious reflections. Yet withal I retained firmness to support me under the pressure of distress. . . . At length I was carried in a litter between two horses, twelve miles, to Kentucky River, where we made a station, and called it Boonsborough, situated in a plain on the south side of the river, wherein was a lick with two sulphur springs strongly impregnated.

On entering the plain we were permitted to view a very interesting and romantic sight. A number of buffaloes, of all sizes, supposed to be between two and three hundred, made off from the lick in every direction; some running, some walking, others loping slowly and carelessly, with young calves playing, skipping, and bounding through the plain. Such a sight some of us never saw before, nor perhaps never may again. . . .

Our military forces, when united, numbered about sixty or sixty-five men, expert riflemen. We lived plentifully on wild meat, buffalo, bear, deer, and turkey, without bread or salt, generally in good health, until the month of July, when I left the country.

Colonel Richard Henderson . . . called an assembly, by election of members, out of our small numbers; organized a government, convened the assembly, in May, 1775, consisting of eighteen members, exclusive of the speaker, passed several laws for the regulation of our little community, well adapted to the policy of an infant government. . . .

This small beginning, that little germ of policy, by a few adventurers from North Carolina, has given birth to the now flourishing State of Kentucky. From that period the population increased with such rapidity, that in less than twenty years it became a state.

Felix Walker, "Narrative of Experiences with Daniel Boon in Kentucky" (1775)

The fort at Knoxville, Tennessee, in the 1700s

AMONG the native animals . . . a buffalo, much resembling a large bull, of a great size, with a large head, thick short crooked horns, and broader in his forepart than behind. Upon his shoulder is a large lump of flesh, covered with a thick boss of long wool and curly hair, of a dark brown color. They do not rise from the ground as our cattle, but spring up at once upon their feet; are of a broad make and clumsy appearance, with short legs, but run fast, and turn not aside for any thing when chased, except a standing tree. They weigh from five to ten hundred-weight, are excellent meat, supplying the inhabitants in many parts with beef, and their hides make good leather. I have heard a hunter assert, he saw above one thousand buffaloes at the Blue Licks at once, so numerous were they before the first settlers had wantonly sported away their lives. There still remains a great number in the exterior parts of the settlement. They feed upon cane and grass, as other cattle, and are innocent harmless creatures.

There are still to be found many deer, elk, and bears within the settlement, and many more on the borders of it. There are also panthers, wildcats, and wolves.

The waters have plenty of beavers, otters, minks, and muskrats; nor are the animals common to other parts wanting, such as foxes, rabbits, squirrels, racoons, groundhogs, polecats, and oppossums.

John Filson,
The Discovery, Settlement and Present State of Kentucky (1784)

WE . . . hunted every day, and prepared a little cottage to defend us from the Winter storms. . . . On the first day of May, 1770, my brother returned home to the settlement by himself, for a new recruit of horses and ammunition, leaving me by myself, without bread, salt, or sugar, without company of my fellow creatures, or even a horse or dog. I confess I never before was under greater necessity of exercising philosophy and fortitude. A few days I passed uncomfortably. The idea of a beloved wife and family, and their anxiety upon the account of my absence and exposed situation, made sensible impressions on my heart. . . .

One day I undertook a tour through the country, and the diversity and beauties of nature I met with in this charming season, expelled every gloomy . . . thought. Just at the close of day . . . I had gained the summit of a commanding ridge, and, looking round with astonishing delight, beheld the ample plains, the beauteous tracts below. On the other hand, I surveyed the famous river Ohio that rolled in silent dignity, marking the western boundary of Kentucky with inconceivable grandeur. At a vast distance I beheld the mountains lift their venerable brows, and penetrate the clouds. All things were still. I kindled a fire near a fountain of sweet water, and feasted on the loin of a buck, which a few hours before I had killed. . . . My roving excursion . . . had fatigued my body, and diverted my imagination. I laid me down to sleep, and I awoke not until the sun had chased away the night.

"The Adventures of Col. Daniel Boon," in John Filson, *The Discovery, Settlement and Present State of Kentucky* (1784)

Shrimp boat at sunset, Hilton Head Island, Georgia

Left: *Louisiana government house and garden*
Above: *Main house at Wormsloe plantation, Georgia*
Below: *A synagogue in Savannah, Georgia*

When I get to be a composer
I'm gonna write me some music about
Daybreak in Alabama
And I'm gonna put the purtiest songs in it
Rising out of the ground like a swamp mist
And falling out of heaven like soft dew.
I'm gonna put some tall tall trees in it
And the scent of pine needles
And the smell of red clay after rain
And long red necks
And poppy colored faces
And big brown arms
And the field daisy eyes
Of black and white black white black people
And I'm gonna put white hands
And black hands and brown and yellow hands
And red clay earth hands in it
Touching everybody with kind fingers
And touching each other natural as dew
In that dawn of music when I
Get to be a composer
And write about daybreak
In Alabama.

Langston Hughes, "Daybreak in Alabama,"
The Panther and the Lash (New York, 1969)

Pastureland in the sun.

Going West

*The first mountain men crawled,
climbed, and hacked their way.
They did it all on foot, through the
Cumberland Gap and into the
wilderness that lay beyond.*

They came by wagon train, pack team, stage coaches, keel boats, prairie schooners, and any other means they could devise. And when they got as far as the maps could lead them, they kept going.

They spread west, hungry to feel in their hands a piece of soil of which they could say, "This is mine."

Immigrants to Nebraska, 1886

Westward bound

Instead of a "promised land, flowing with milk and honey," some early settlers found buffalo grass and rattlesnakes in the great American prairie. They battled the drought and the grasshopper plagues, fought the long, lean winters, prairie fires, and dust storms. But they were free men now, and the mix of heritage, place, and opportunity began to work. They, too, had a chance at the promise.

From Mary Pearsal's journal, 1851: "Chilled to the bones, starving and the wagon broken down. We'll stay here 'til the spring, hunting for game. Lord oh Lord, why did we come?"

Above and below: *Settlers and sod houses in the Dakota Territory, late 1800s*

Lured by the offer of free land and a chance to start life anew, former slaves from Kentucky, Tennessee, and Indiana formed emigrant trains and headed west to Kansas, to a place called Nicodemus. Leaflets advertised: "All colored people that want to go to Kansas Sept. 5, 1877, can do so for five dollars." More than five hundred came in the years after the Civil War. They worked to fulfill the promise. Nicodemus, named after a legendary slave, was thriving. The newspaper Western Cyclone *reported in 1887: "The streets of the town were daily filled with strange faces. It was difficult to find a residential building."*

THE PEOPLE that came to Nicodemus came out of slavery. They had an old four-room schoolhouse, but they didn't have but two teachers and they just used two rooms. Part of the time they just had one teacher. . . . As far as any entertainment was concerned, the church had socials. They had literary societies then. Now at these literary societies you could get up and give a reading. They called them Declamations. You could learn a reading, commit it to memory, then get up and speak it, or you could sing, if you had some song. You didn't have to be religious. You could sing popular songs if you wanted to. . . .

The slave owners didn't give 'em one penny and not a crust of bread when they kicked 'em out and told 'em they were free, and what little they gained they worked for other people between that time and the time of coming to Nicodemus. And, you know, my grandmother had nine children. There wasn't much she could save. . . .

They started out with five or six acres of ground and then they increased it as people began to get horses. They could raise squash, potatoes, turnips, and through the summer they had green vegetables. They learned how to bury beets, cabbage,

and potatoes and keep them all winter. I remember when my parents used to make a potato hole, a cabbage hole. You dig a big hole in the ground, pretty deep, depending on how many things you were gonna put in it, and then you would put in prairie hay. Then you put in a layer of potatoes, and cover that up with some more hay and then put dirt on top of that, and then when you wanted potatoes, see, you dug and put the dirt back again, and take it all back, and then put the hay back and then reach in and get whatever potatoes you wanted. The potatoes stayed fresh. They didn't grow, they're just nice. The cabbage you'd do the same.

Mrs. Ola Scruggs Wilson
Nicodemus, Kansas
April, 1973

THE FIRST settlers had dugouts. Now, these dugouts, they were built in the ground. Oh, maybe the top of it, the top of it might just be about that high. They dug a hole in the ground and then they cut steps down to it, to get in. You see, you had a door down where the rooms were, or room—they didn't have rooms, room. It could be ever so big but it just had the one door and sometimes they put a window in the end above ground, and then that give you one little dim light when the weather was cold. Because they didn't have glass in the door, they had wooden something, probably the doors were made out of wood. Just made. There were some carpenters in the bunch. Stonemasons, brickmasons.

Mrs. Ola Scruggs Wilson
Nicodemus, Kansas
April, 1973

Dakota pioneers

For a long time the great rivers and canals carried people west, and cities like Buffalo and Pittsburgh, St. Louis, St. Joe, and Cincinnati became the starting points.

From an advertisement in a midwestern newspaper: "The proprietor of these boats, having maturely considered the many inconveniences and dangers incident to navigating the Ohio, has taken great pains to render the accommodations on board the boat as agreeable and convenient as they can possibly be made. No danger need be apprehended from

the enemy, as every person on board will be under cover, made proof to rifle balls, and with convenient portholes for firing out."

Finally came the long trek overland by wagon train. And for everyone, no matter what their reason for deciding to make the journey, there was a knowledge that they were leaving behind both comfort and all sense of civilization. Their lives would depend upon ingenuity, self-reliance, and the advice of those who had gone before.

Sod house on the plains, 1884

Our house, plaster and all, grew on our own land. We took clay from the hillside, where we dug a cellar, and sand and water from the creek. We made the mortar–the trowel out of an old piece of plow to put it with. I think we'll come out all right.

Diary of a Nebraska settler

There were those who saw the great heartland plains—the seemingly endless, flat lands—as being without value.

Edwin James wrote in 1819: "I do not hesitate in giving the opinion that the land is almost unfit for cultivation, and of course uninhabitable."

Pedro de Castañeda, the historian of Coronado's epic exploration of the Southwest, complained, "The plains consist of nothing but cows" —his description of buffalo; and he thought it strange that the Indians of the plains lived alone, sustaining themselves entirely from the buffalo.

Opposite: *Early pioneer outpost* Below: *Leavenworth,
Kansas, in the early days*
Bottom: *Mining town in the Dakota Territory, 1888*

Two laws opened the West, the Homestead Act and the Railroad Bill of 1862, ironic footnotes to the great crises of Lincoln's administration that were generated by the Emancipation Proclamation. And to the West came those who never before had held a franchise to own land. From a tragic history of slavery and degradation they came to the hardships of the new land.

Driving the Golden Spike, 1869

Here and there a lawyer came, here and there a doctor. And here and there across the West came little towns, settled places. Wherever the railroad stopped, there would be six or seven houses —places like Abilene, Kansas, tail end of a spur on the Union Pacific Railroad.

The great iron horse symbolizes the driving energy of a young America and her abiding resolve that the land would be tamed, settled, and prosperous. Here, it was said, was the way to open the frontiers. Here was the great spiderweb of rails, rooted to the earth by work gangs numbering in the tens of thousands. And all around the tracks cutting up the plains, hunters slaughtered buffalo to supply the men who made the railroads.

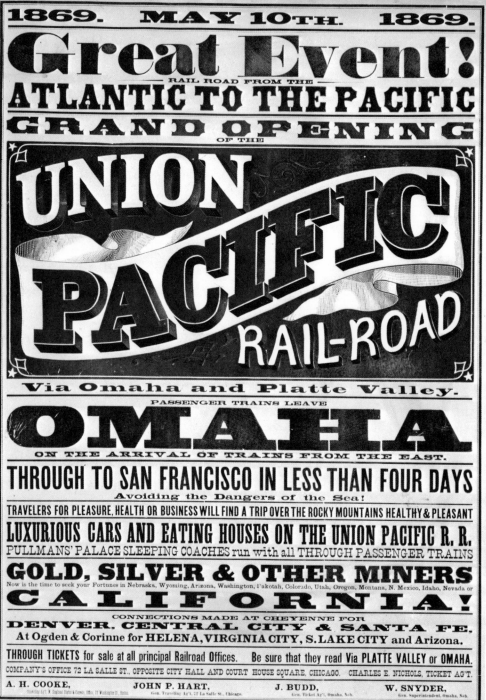

Pounds of beef, carloads of hogs coming in, being shipped out all over the world. This is what people here have always known: that Omaha, the city, exists because of the land. The yards that gave jobs to sixteen thousand men at a time and brought the shopkeepers to sell them clothes, the saloon keepers and the gamblers to fill their pleasures, the lawyers to write their wills, the police to guard their homes, the railmen to ship their goods, and the doctors to deliver their babies. What is the country but its people?

Omaha was born on land speculation in 1854. Under United States government law, any settler had a right to claim land. And the early days saw a small group of

The Nebraska Territorial Legislature in session

men make claim to thousands of acres and then start selling it for profit. But in Omaha City in the mid-1850s, all who came were subject to the rules of the Omaha City Claim Club.

The Claim Club passed a resolution that no man should be permitted to preempt land. Any settler exercising his legal right to homesteader claim in Omaha would be disposed of.

Some squatters were tied to trees, threatened at gunpoint, or simply escorted out of town. There was the case of a man named Callahan. The records show he was arrested by the Claim Club and brought before the members for a hearing, in which he was given thirty minutes to decide whether to give up his claim or be drowned in the Missouri River.

South Omaha Union Stockyards and packing houses

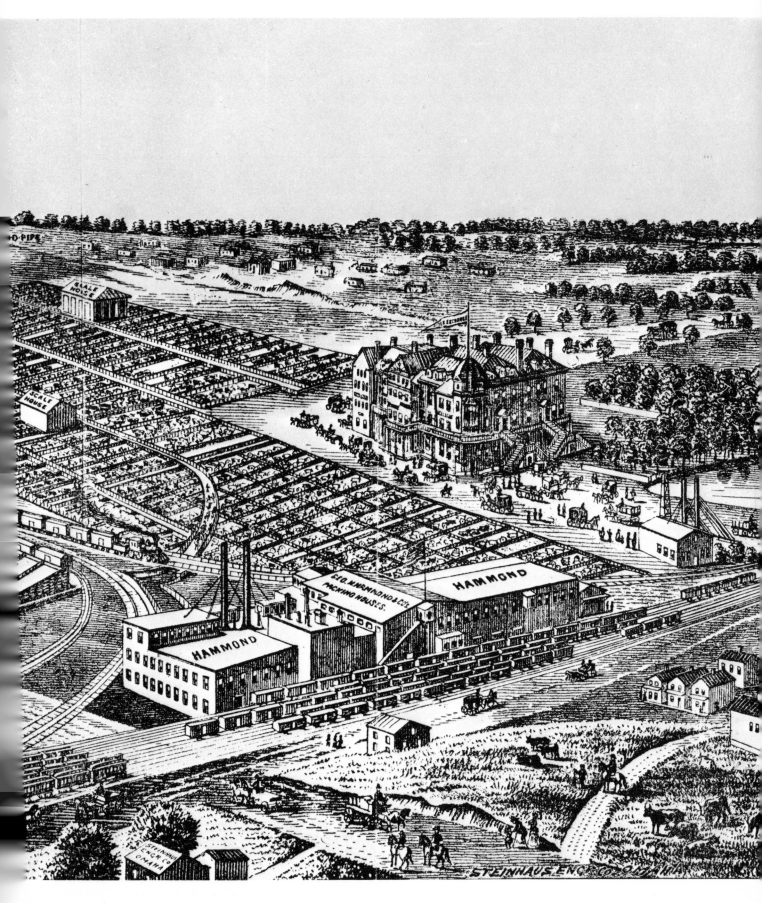

*In the first days of her founding
there were only people who worked
the land because they had to—
because it held the sustenance of
survival. These are the beginnings
that gave us our heritage: the
American romance with the land,
the start of the American idea.*

Opposite: *The Cumberland Gap, looking west from Kentucky*
Following pages: *A Minnesota farmstead*

Above: *Working the land, near Omaha, Nebraska*

Above: *The rolling farmland of Nebrask*

Left: *Cattle in the Omaha stockyards*

Winter on the range (above) *and an abandoned farmstead* (right), *both in Utah*

Acoma Pueblo, New Mexico

In New Mexico, the facade of an adobe church
(above) *and a church and graveyard* (below)

Following pages: *Forest in the*
mountains of Colorado

WHO CAN say when this region will once again be covered by the waters of the deep? Geologically, speaking, it is not so long ago that it rose from the sea. Its mountain slopes are almost as treacherous as the icy sea in which, by the way, one scarcely ever sees a sailboat or a hardy swimmer, though one does occasionally spot a seal, an otter, or a sperm whale. The sea, which looks so near and so tempting, is often difficult to reach. We know that the Conquistadores were unable to make their way along the coast, neither could they cut through the brush which covers the mountain slopes. An inviting land, but hard to conquer. It seeks to remain unspoiled, uninhabited by man.

Often, when following the trail which meanders over the hills, I pull myself up in an effort to encompass the glory and the grandeur which envelops the whole horizon. Often, when the clouds pile up in the north and the sea is churned with whitecaps, I say to myself: "This is the California that men dreamed of years ago, this is the Pacific that Balboa looked out on from the Peak of Darien, this is the face of the earth as the Creator intended it to look."

Henry Miller, *Big Sur*
(New York, 1957)

Opposite: *The Pacific Northwest coast*

The Indian

The American Indian is of the soil
—for the hand that fashioned the
continent also fashioned the man
for his surroundings. He once grew
as naturally as the wild sunflowers;
he belongs just as the buffalo
belonged. In the Indian, the spirit
of the land is still vested; it will be
until other men are able to divine
and meet its rhythm.

Luther Standing Bear
Oglala Sioux Chief

From the beginning man was awed by the West. The American Indian, the first to see the land, expressed his reverence by linking his life to all the forces of nature.

For Comanche, Apache, Sioux, and Cheyenne the plains were home, and they moved comfortably in accommodation to its seasons. It has been estimated that there were ten million Indians in the United States before the European colonists arrived. Within a few short years there would be only 250,000 remaining, mostly on the plains. Chief Standing Bear explains part of the reason:

"We did not think of the great open plain as wild. To us it was tame, surrounded by the blessings of the great mystery.

"Only to the white man was nature a wilderness and only to him was the land infested with wild animals and savage people."

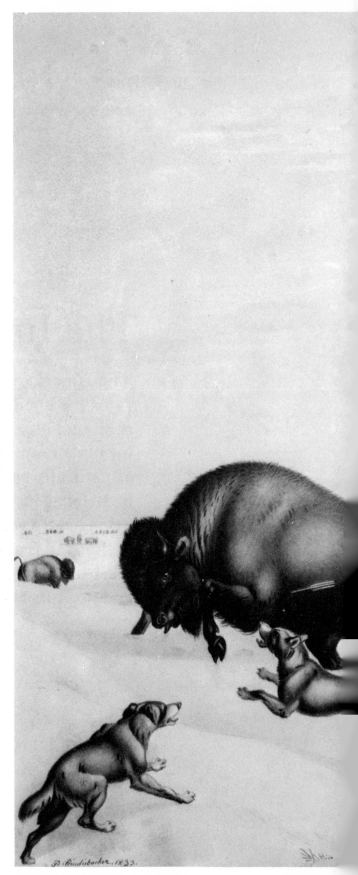

Blackfoot hunting on snowshoes

Of the many solemn treaties that had been made between the sovereign Indian nations and the United States of America, Red Cloud, the Dakota Sioux chief, would say: "They made us many promises, more than I can remember, but they never kept but one. They promised to take our land, and they took it."

Photo. and copyright 1891, by Grabill,
Deadwood, S. D.

Despairing of the vanished wildlife upon which the Indians depended, Bear Tooth of the Crow Tribe spoke out with passion:

"Fathers, Fathers, Fathers, hear me well. Call back your young men. They have run over our country. They have destroyed the growing wood and the green grass, they have set fire to our lands. Fathers, your young men have devastated the country and killed my animals, the elk, the deer, my buffalo.

"Fathers, if I went into your country to kill your animals, what would you say? Should I not be wrong and would you not make war on me?"

It might have been the mount of a fallen Spanish soldier or a spirited stallion, or restless mares—one by one, they ran from the battlefields, broke out of the corrals, found each other, and began a new life in the wild, shedding armor and trappings for bridles of wind and saddles of sun.

But they were too beautiful, too strong to stay free. The Indian saw the horse, first with fear, then with longing, and the union of the Indian and the horse is the image engraved on the face of the West. Greatly valued in hunting and warfare, horses soon became among the most prized possessions of the southwest Plains Indians. Many songs were written in their honor. Among the most beautiful is the Navajo Horse Song:

My horse has a hoof like a striped
    agate.
His fetlock is like a fine eagle
    plume,
His legs are like quick lightning.
My horse has a tail like a trailing
    black cloud.
I am wealthy because of him.
Before me peaceful, behind me
    peaceful,
Over me peaceful, under me
    peaceful.
All around me peaceful—
Peaceful voice when he neighs.
I am everlasting and peaceful.
I stand for my horse.

There are ceremonies in Indian religion today seemingly as old as creation itself—ceremonies for the corn, for rain, for healing, for a newborn child. In the country of the Navajo, a medicine man begins the day-and-a-half-long ceremony for a newborn child with the digging of the root of a yucca plant.

Korosta Katzina Song (Hopi)

Yellow butterflies,
Over the blossoming virgin corn,

With pollen-painted faces
Chase one another in brilliant throng.

Blue butterflies,
Over the blossoming virgin beans,
With pollen-painted faces
Chase one another in brilliant streams.

Medicine mask dance

Over the blossoming beans,
Over the virgin beans
Wild bees hum.

Over your field of growing corn
    All day shall hang the thunder-cloud:
Over your field of growing corn
    All day shall come the rushing rain.

Mary Roberts Coolidge,
*The Rainmakers: Indians of
Arizona and New Mexico* (Boston, 1929)

I   Here I am sitting with my power
     I bring the South Wind toward me.
     After the wind I draw the clouds
     And after the clouds I draw the rain
          that makes the wild flowers grow on our home
            ground
          and look so beautiful.

II   By the sandy water I breathe in the odor of the sea
     From there the wind comes and blows over the world.
     By the sandy water I breathe in the odor of the sea
     From there the clouds come and rain falls over the
          world.

III   The cottonwood leaves are falling and flying in the air.
     On top of the remaining mountain, they are flying around
     And falling as though they were wet.

IV   Under us the world spreads wide
     From there the corn grows up
     On the leaves the water moves in little drops.
     Under us the mountain stands wide
     And the water spreads over the vines.

Mary Roberts Coolidge,
*The Rainmakers: Indians of
Arizona and New Mexico* (Boston, 1929)

Through ten thousand years or more a unique culture evolved. The rituals still practiced today reflect the Indians' way of life.

THE SNAKE CEREMONIAL, one of the most archaic rites among the Pueblos, was probably widespread in the Southwest. . . .

Just before sunset we climbed from our camp to the top of the mesa and for a brief hour absorbed that atmosphere of ineffable quiet which lies at nightfall upon the desert and the far mauve and blue mountain rim. Only the sound of a sleepy fowl or a whimpering child, the faint moccasined footfalls of passing villagers, and the ticktack of burros pattering up the rocky trail broke the stillness. The snowy thunderheads, which had been piling up all the afternoon, turned rosy and paused before the setting sun.

As the moments passed, little black figures appeared on the desert—naked, trotting along wearily. With a pouch of snakes at the thigh and a prayer plume in the hand, they mounted the trail, bringing the last of their capture to be used on the morrow. Each priest paused at the top of the mesa, turned his face to the west, and made his obeisance to the Sun, the giver of life and fertility. . . .

Each of the nine ceremonial days has secret traditional rites, culminating in the Antelope Race on the eighth morning, the Snake Society Race on the ninth morning, and the final joint public ceremony of the snake handling on the ninth afternoon. . . .

On the second day the Snake priests go out in pairs to hunt snakes, provided with digging-sticks, snake whips of feathers, and pouches of buckskin. They follow the usual ceremonial circuit of the Hopis—north, west, south, east—during four successive days. . . . One half or more of the sixty to eighty snakes required are rattlesnakes. The remainder are racers, whip and bull snakes.

The snakes are usually found by following their trails in the dust. . . . At nightfall the Snake priests . . . deposit their snakes in pottery vessels in the kiva. . . .

At daylight on the ninth day two of the Snake priests dress as warriors. They carry a bull-roarer or whizzer made of sticks, which when twirled makes a noise like falling rain; and a curious lightning-shooter of crossed sticks. . . . [They] go down onto the plain a mile or two from the village. Here the messenger who brought water from a sacred spring the day before deposits prayer sticks and makes prayers at four places some distance apart. When the warrior-priests reach the fourth and farthest spot, the runners, who are already lined up for the contest, start toward the pueblo. The first one who passes the messenger is given a gourd in a net containing the water from the sacred spring, which he in turn must pass on to any runner who goes by him. As the runners approach the goal of the mesa, they are joined, on the morning of the ninth day, by the Snake priests. . . . The winner of the race receives as a prize the gourd of water and a small ring which he buries in his field, which are to ensure a good crop. . . .

At last, when the sun is low in the west, the Snake Dance begins. The Antelope priests file out and after circling the plaza stand in line awaiting the Snake priests. . . . They circle the plaza three times, each stamping on a plank in front of the cottonwood bower, the *kisi,* to notify the denizens of the Underworld that a ceremony in their honor is progressing. They face the Antelope chorus, the rattles tremble with a sound like the warning of the rattlesnake, and a deep, low-toned chant begins like a distant storm. The chant increases in volume, the lines sway, then undulate backward and forward, and at last in a culminating burst of the chant, the Snake men form in groups of three and dance around the plaza. . . .

As the trios in succession arrive before the *kisi* the carrier drops to his knees, secures a snake which he grasps in his mouth, rises, and dances around in a circular path four times, when the snake is dropped to the ground and is picked up with lightning rapidity by the third member of the trio who retains the squirming reptile in his hands.

When all the snakes have been handled, the head priest makes a large circle of corn flour, drawing six radii which represent the six world regions. Into this circle the snakes are thrown in a heap, and a group of girls and women, who have been standing ready with baskets of meal, sprinkle the snakes and the dancers with it. At a given signal, the Snake priests approach, grab as many snakes out of the heap as they can hold, run down to the plain, and release them.

As soon as the ceremony is over, the priests retire to the kivas to remove their costumes and then go to the edge of the mesa for the purification rite. . . . Four days of games and festivities follow, and, if the ceremony has been successful in bringing abundant rain, the people are altogether happy. . . .

The Hopis have medicine women as well as medicine men, and the most important of these was . . . Saalako, the Mother of the Snake Priest. She brewed the dark medicine used for purification after the Snake Dance and guarded the secret of the antidotes for snake bites. . . .

At sunset the Snake Dance is ended. The crowds of the curious depart, some subdued by this touch of the primitive and mysterious, but most of them still hysterically discussing what they have seen with the eye but have not comprehended with the spirit. . . . Again the desert hush comes over the Hopi land. The traditions are once more fulfilled, the gods must certainly be satisfied, since thunder-clouds have covered the face of Father Sky.

Mary Roberts Coolidge,
*The Rainmakers: Indians of
Arizona and New Mexico* (Boston, 1929)

Prayer for Rain (from the Pueblo of Sia)

White floating clouds,
Clouds like the plains,
Come and water the earth.
Sun embrace the earth
That she may be fruitful.
Moon, lion of the north,
Bear of the west,
Badger of the south,
Wolf of the east,
Eagle of the heavens
Shrew of the earth,
Elder war hero,
Warriors of the six mountains of the world,
Intercede with the cloud people for us,
That they may water the earth.
Medicine bowl, cloud bowl, and water vase
Give us your hearts,
That the earth may be watered.

I make the ancient road of meal,
That my song may pass over it—
The ancient road.
White shell bead woman
Who lives where the sun goes down,
Mother Whirlwind,
Father Sus'sistinnako,
Mother Ya'ya, creator of good thoughts.
Yellow woman of the north,
Blue woman of the west,
Red woman of the south,
White woman of the east,
Slightly yellow woman of the zenith,
And dark woman of the nadir,
I ask your intercession with the cloud
   people.

Mary Roberts Coolidge,
*The Rainmakers: Indians of
Arizona and New Mexico* (Boston, 1929)

THIS IS Navajo land; we never did leave it. I got great-great-grandpop buried here and my grandfather on my father's side and my father. My mother comes from the Utes in Colorado, but she can remember that her great-great-grandfather was hit and didn't go on the Long Walk and stayed in the canyon instead. So now really nobody could take this land away from us. It's for all the children and the great-grandchildren. My daughter Sheila's naval cord is buried here so that she'll always have the right to come back to the reservation.

My mother, Abbie Laughter, is named Donnaba, which means "made in the war." My father was a medicine man and I've always followed the old ways to some extent. A medicine man blessed me before I had Sheila, so now he'll bless her in a ceremony that lasts a day and a night. In the morning she'll be washed with yucca soap and dried with cornmeal, and then her grandmother will take her out and hold her up to the sun, saying a little prayer for her: "Let this child be from the north, from the west, from the south, from the east." The medicine man will bless each part of her body and talk about the sacred mountains and gods. Sheila will be called her Navajo name, Donnaba, and there'll be singing all night in the hogan.

I'll raise my daughter both in the Anglo way and my own traditional way. She's going to learn to speak Navajo and English. I hope she'll have respect for the Navajo as I did and that someday she'll be recognized as a Navajo and an Indian somewhere off the reservation.

For a while it seemed our traditions were fading, but now there's a school at Rough Rock teaching the Navajo ways again. They're teaching the ceremonies and arts and crafts like silver working. If you leave the reservation and see something made by the Navajos, it makes you feel proud to know what your people can do. My mother raised so many of us just by depending on what she knows, like weaving rugs and making pottery and baskets to sell to the trading post. She took care of the sheep, too, sometimes riding and other times on foot. She's seventy-seven and still works all the time. My father was paid in sheep or jewelry as well as money, so that's how we got along.

We always had a traditional hogan of mud and sand, because it stayed warm in winter once the fire was going and cool in summer. If we built a house or modern hogan of lumber, which my mother likes, we always had to have our traditional hogan alongside for my father.

In the springtime we shear the sheep. The natural colors of the wool are black, gray, white, and sometimes brown. If you want other colors you use herbs or plants to get them. Store-bought dye is usually red. When the yarn is spun and the loom set up, my mother just starts weaving what she's thinking about. A lot of the rugs tell a story, but even if it's just a diamond pattern, you don't ever go by a book. I'm going to put a loom in our trailer for Sheila to learn on.

The main thing about the ceremonies and traditions is that they refresh your mind. You don't think about your sheep too much anymore. You don't think about your horse too much anymore. The songs let you come back again like when you used to live here with your family. We'll do the singing over Sheila so she'll start thinking about horses and sheep and her grandparents here on the reservation. When she's a teen-ager and ready to leave us, maybe she'll remember that a long time ago the medicine man blessed her. Then she'll remember she's a Navajo.

Irene Smith
Navajo Nation, Arizona
March, 1973

Irene Smith's mother, Abbie Laughter (above),
and a Navajo medicine man (below), *both at the*
Kayenta Reservation, Arizona

Opposite: *Modern farm plot and ancient*
dwelling at the Canyon de Chelly, Arizona

If the white man were a wise people, when he first set foot in the Western Hemisphere, when he first met a Native American, he would have asked him this: "How long have you been here?"

And Mr. Indian would have said, "For as long as there have been stars in the sky and sands on the beaches."

The white man would have said, "You have done well, for this country is in a beautiful state." And Mr. Indian would have said, "It is as it was in the beginning."

And then the white man, if he was truly a wise man, would have said, "Teach me your ways so that I, too, can keep this land as it was in the beginning."

Russel Means, Oglala Sioux
Pine Ridge Reservation, South Dakota
June, 1973

Opposite: *Ruins of cliff dwellings at Canyon de Chelly, Arizona*

The Cowboy

It was in 1843 that an Englishman, William Ballaert, visited San Antonio, Texas, and first saw a new kind of American, later to be called the cowboy.

The American cowboy became a folk hero because we mold our legends to suit ourselves. We've made him what we want him to be—a memorial to a way of life that flourished when the American frontier seemed to stretch from the Mississippi to forever.

There are those who say that when the West filled with people something important was taken from the life of the country. Without a frontier, what was left?

Abilene became a place where the long drive ended and a cowboy could cut loose.

"We'll hit the town.
And we hit her on the fly.
We bedded down the cattle
On a hill nearby."

Saloons, cafes, easy ladies and headstrong gunmen—a trail town, a lawless, raucous celebration of the toughest kind of man. That was Abilene—and Wichita—and Dodge, where lawmen held the cowboy at bay. Among them: Luke Short, Bat Masterson, and Wyatt Earp.

The last of the cattle drives went north. With the plains stripped of buffalo, General Sheridan's words became prophetic:

"Your prairies can be filled with cattle, and the cowboy will follow the hunter as a second forerunner of an advanced civilization."

Above: *On the trail*
Right: *Branding the cattle*

Texas cattle, the Longhorns, grew fat on the ranges of the Panhandle, waiting for the Civil War to end and shipments east to start again. They were worth three dollars a head in Texas, but in Kansas City and St. Louis the price was thirty or forty dollars. The problem was getting them there, through Indian territory and past the hazardous plains. And here the cowboy made his legend—on those incredible odysseys along old wagon routes, like trader Jesse Chisolm's road to Kansas.

Abilene, a forgotten spur on the Union Pacific, could thank Joe McCoy's ingenuity for making it the target of the Texas cattle drives. He built the stockyards and sent out word to Texas: "Get me your cattle, I'll get you your money."

In 1843 an Englishman called them "a rude, uncultivated race of beings, who pass the greater part of their lives in the saddle, herding cattle and horses . . . unused to comfort and regardless alike of ease and danger, they have a hardy sunburnt appearance."

There were all kinds of men in the cow camps of the territories, and all nationalities: blacks, Mexicans, and Anglo-Americans.

Among them was a large group who had fled from the States to escape problems or prosecution. It would be years before the romance of the cowboy made itself felt. At the start they were ranch hands, scratching a living on small, isolated, self-contained spreads.

IN THE SPRING of 1878 I traded one of my horses for a saddle and a six-shooter and started out to catch up with a herd that would be at Fort Griffin about the twenty-third of May. . . . There was a good post there, with four hundred soldiers and a small town. . . . The night before I got to the post I stayed at a cow ranch. . . . We had supper, and after everything had been cleaned up one of the men spread a blanket on the dirt floor, hauled out a deck of cards, and told us to get in. There were two men and a boy about 18. . . . Each of the men had six-shooters, but had hung them on the wall when they came in to supper. I told the fellow that I could not play cards and he did not insist, but told the boy to sit in. The boy proceeded to get out his money. . . . [He] had about $40, but in an hour he didn't have a cent. Then he wanted to quit, but the others said the game must go on. The boy insisted that he had no more money. . . . The men said he had two good horses and a saddle and with that talk the boy sat in again. One of the men put up his horse against the boy's horse and finally won both of them. The boy then wanted to quit, but they told him he still had a good saddle and they would put up $25 against it and give the boy the deal. The boy brought in a good saddle and I began to feel sorry for him and said: "Oh, boys, don't take his saddle away from him." The dark fellow gave me a wicked look and said: "You better attend to your own business and let mine alone."

I slipped out and went to bed. The next morning the boy told me he had been out there a year and had got some money and two good horses and was going to Fort Worth with those steers and then go home. He said his mother had a little farm and was getting along poorly and he had written her that he would soon be at home with some money and two good horses. Then he said: "I can't go home now. I think I will borrow some kind of an old saddle and a horse and go to work again."

. . . After things cooled down and there was no one around, the man on the job, who was about fifty years old, one-eyed and very thin, said . . . "Now, as you seem to be a stranger, just like I was once, I will give you a little advice. . . . The men you see around here are one- and two-time men killers and I would not go about with them. You can swim the river and catch the herd tonight, and I would do that."

I had just fifty cents and I bought a biscuit or two and a small piece of bacon and made for the river. I got across, soaked, and everything in the pack was soaked. This was one of the important rivers of Texas, the Brazos. This was the twenty-fifth of May, 1879. I was now in Throckmorton County and there was nothing in sight. There were no settlements from here to Indian Territory, 150 miles away, and many wild Indians. I poured the water out of my boots while the horses grazed and then took the trail where the herd had gone. This was a fine range country and this was about the only herd that had gone across there. . . . There were then 1,500 big steers, 1,500 cows, and 1,850 steer yearlings. . . .

The cattle scattered out, so they did not make a very distinct trail and I lost it, being so busy looking for Indians. I stopped on the bank of a pretty little creek where the grass and water were good and where there was a large grove of elm trees. I broiled my bacon on a stick, but my bread and coffee got soaked while I was crossing the river and were not fit to eat. When it grew dark I hobbled two of my horses and tied the other to a mesquite tree at my head, giving him plenty of rope to graze. I lay down to sleep with a gun in my hand. I was pretty much of a tenderfoot these days. . . . About two in the morning it began to rain and I got up and sat against the mesquite tree. I had gone to sleep again when lightning struck one of those elms. I reared back just as the horse jerked the small tree, which

Huffman, NEW STUDIO, Miles City,
✠
Graham Block, Montana.

took all the hide off the back of my head. It rained hard then, with a north wind blowing, and I could hear the cattle bawling a few miles north. I think that was the most dismal night I ever spent.

Pioneering in Texas and Wyoming: Incidents in the Life of James C. Shaw

THE GENUINE specimen of a Western cowboy is beyond description, and is only to be seen to be admired.

His dress generally consists of "chaps," which are a peculiar kind of leather leggings reaching to the hips and covering the whole of the legs, with a ragged fringe of thongs hanging from the outside seams, a red or blue flannel shirt, and a large slouch hat, ornamented with a dried rattlesnake skin or other strange band.

Add to this somewhat startling attire, a gaudy handkerchief, loosely tied round the neck, a belt, with bowie-knife and brace of pistols, not forgetting an enormous pair of Spanish spurs, and you have something of the dress, which, when put on a handsome figure, in the shape of a dashing fellow with long waving hair hanging to his shoulders, and a carefully cultivated military moustache, presents one of the most fascinating and romantic pictures to be imagined.

As a rule, the cowboy proper has been nothing else from his youth, and would not be, if he had the finest opportunities.

He lives mostly in the open air, and is the most reckless, devil-may-care, light-hearted man to be met with in creation; ever ready to help a friend, or resent an insult, and as free with his money as his pistol.

Unlike most boys in America, he does not aspire to be President, and the height of his ambition is to be boss cowboy, and never to be beaten at anything pertaining to his profession, the art of which is chiefly riding and throwing the lasso. In a word, his virtues are many, and his vices few, the worst of the latter being the propensity for gambling and shooting. . . .

Snuffin' Ranch was on the banks of the river, which is a broad shallow stream, fed by the melting snows from the Rocky Mountains. The home ranch consisted of about 640 acres, running along the bank of the river, and extending back about a quarter of a mile from the edge of the high-water mark. It was enclosed by a stout barbed wire fence, and inside were kept the milch cows, the horses used on the ranch, and those required by the boys.

The house, instead of being built of wood, was constructed of sods, laid one on top of the other, and lined inside with wood. This forms the best kind of house, as the walls are of great thickness, and keep out the cold in winter and the heat in summer; besides being a solid mass, more stable than masonry. . . .

The walls of the corral, stable, and outhouses were all built of a similar material, and in the same way. The process of obtaining the sods and building in this fashion is as follows: whilst the ground is moist from the rain, the turf, or sod, in the bottom land near the river, is ploughed up, so as to cut it off clean from the ground, and is then cut into blocks of an equal size, carried away, and built up, one on top of another. In a short time they are united together.

"Bunny," *Two Years a Cowboy* (London, 1887)

WHEN we got into Texas we found the country very new. . . . We went into Hopkins County to Blackjack Grove, where we had heard of a Mr. Hart that had some cattle. . . . When we came to the place I saw two or three fine-looking men but could see nothing else except a log cabin surrounded by a high fence. I inquired if this was where Mr. Hart lived. The gentleman said he did not know of such a man in the country. I told him . . . [that] as we had missed our way, and were strangers in the country, we would like to stay with him. He told us to turn our horses into the yard and feed them. When we went in the house for supper I told him I was very sorry we had missed our way and that I thought he must certainly know Mr. Hart. He said we were perfectly welcome to stay and take what they had. His wife was gone but would be home in the morning; she had gone to visit a sick neighbor, about sixteen miles away. They shucked the corn and ground the meal on a steel mill, which I helped them do.

Before we went to bed the gentleman said: "Probably it was Merida Hart that you were inquiring for?"

I said: "Yes, sir, that is the man."

"Well, that is my name; there are no Mr.'s in this country."

. . . In the morning Mr. Hart took us across the country to see the cattle and to call upon some of his neighbors. We did not make any trade with Mr. Hart; he was too high. He asked us what we did with the cattle when we took them to the north. I told him we fed them on corn and would have about three hogs to every two steers to pick up the droppings. He asked what the droppings were, and I told him after the cattle would eat the corn, what passed through them the hogs would eat and get fat on.

"Well," he said, "I have heard you Yankees were very close people, but I did not suppose you were so close that you would try to fatten hogs on the same feed as the cattle." . . .

On our way back we had to cross Red River. . . . I started back into another part of the country and about the middle of the day I met a white man, with a wagon load of pecan nuts. His wagon wheel had broken, and he had nothing with which to mend it, but his ax and pocket knife. . . . He told me I could get some cattle of a man by the name of Pussly. . . .

Pussly had a beautiful place. . . . His father was an Englishman. He had died when his son was quite young and before this tribe of Indians had crossed over on the west side of the Mississippi. When he learned I was an Englishman he and his family treated me as if I was related to them. I purchased about eighty head of very fine steers, giving nine dollars a head for them. I think the cattle would have weighed in the neighborhood of twelve hundred pounds. . . .

It rained quite a good deal and we found the river and creeks had all raised. We camped one night on the bank of a stream and the next morning found it had raised nineteen feet; of course the river was not very wide. . . . When we got to the Arkansas River, about fifteen miles west from Fort Gibson, we got some Indians to help us and built a raft of logs to float our wagon over the river. We kept the cattle back until we had completed the rafts, which was about twelve o'clock; then we got the Indians to help us and drove the cattle into the river, making them swim across. . . . As I could not swim I got an Indian to ride beside me, so if I was thrown off he could take care of me. I dared not say anything, for there were others in the same fix; a little timid. The river where we crossed was about half a mile wide. Sometimes we would come to a sand bar and the horses would wade some distance; then swim again; then strike another sand bar, and so on.

. . . I sat on my horse every night while we were coming through the Indian country; I was so afraid something would scare the cattle that I could not sleep in the tent; but we had no stampede. When we got into Missouri, about seventy or eighty miles, we struck the trail we had gone to Texas on. The first town we came to was Springfield, where we had stopped on our way down to have our horses shod. At this place I found some mail and a little money that had been collected for me in Wisconsin. . . . The Landlord . . . insisted that my partner and I should

come and take dinner with him and his friends and tell them about our trip; in those days people did not know as much about Texas as the people of the present day do of Japan.

Life of Tom Candy Ponting (1907)

Ask any man who ever made a trip over the trail if he was ever caught on the plains in a rainstorm, and did he really enjoy saturated clothing and wet blankets. Ask him if he ever worked in the north and in the eye of a blizzard rode to turn a winter drift of cattle, and was lifted out of the saddle, benumbed with cold, and did he really feel the occupation was a romantic one. If still unsatisfied, ask him from a sanitary standpoint if there was anything would beat spreading his clothing on an anthill to remove the vermin.

Andy Adams, *The Log of a Cowboy* (Boston, 1903)

An old-time cowboy, looking back over the years, once said of his fellows: "I and they were but creatures of circumstance—the circumstance of an unfenced world."

The world no longer is unfenced, and in the age of technology many of the old ways of cowboying have passed or changed. Yet here and there, out in the range lands of the western United States, are pockets that have resisted time—pockets where life and cowboying are much the same as they were at the end of the last century.

A Texas cowboy shields his eyes against the sun.

Top: *Rodeo at the Pitchfork Ranch, Dickens, Texas*
Above: *A quiet moment at the Omaha stockyard*
Right: *Cowboys on a Texas ranch*
Following pages: *Cowboys driving the herd, Texas*

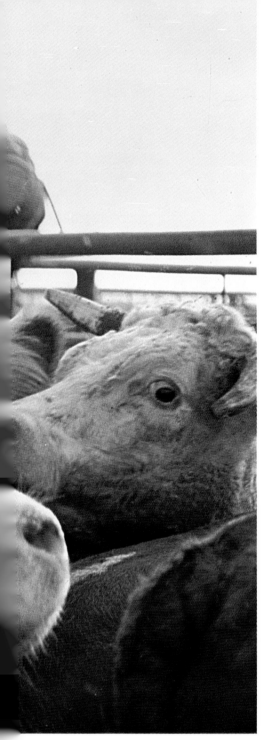

Left and below: *Rounding up the cattle at the Pitchfork Ranch, Dickens, Texas*
Bottom: *Texas cowboys wearing chaps*

Whoopee Ti-yi-yo

As I walked out one morning for
    pleasure,
I spied a young cowpoke a-riding
    along;
His hat was thrown back and his
    spurs were a-jingling,
    And as he approached he was
    singing this song:

Refrain:
Whoopee ti-yi-yo, get along, little
    dogies,
    It's your misfortune and none
    of my own.
Whoopee ti-yi-yo, get along, little
    dogies,
    For you know that Wyoming
    will be your new home.

It's early in springtime we round
    up the dogies,
    We mark them and brand them
    and bob off their tails;
We round up our horses and load
    the chuck wagon,
    Then throw those little dogies
    upon the trail.
(*Refrain*)

It's whooping and yelling and
    driving the dogies;
    Oh, how I wish they would
    hurry along.

It's whooping and punching, get on,
    little dogies,
    For you know that Wyoming
    will be your new home.
(*Refrain*)

Some boys they go on the trail for
    pleasure,
    But that's where they get it
    most awfully wrong;
For you've no idea of the trouble
    they give us
    While we go driving those
    dogies along.
(*Refrain*)

When nighttime comes and we
    hold them on the bed-ground,
    Those dear little dogies that roll
    on so slow,
Round up the herd and cut out the
    stray yearlings
    And roll the little dogies that
    never rolled before.
(*Refrain*)

Opposite: *One of the children at the Dowse Ranch, Custer County, Nebraska*

The Immigrant

So at last I was going to
America! Really, really going,
at last! The boundaries burst.
The arch of heaven soared.
A million suns shone out for
every star. The winds rushed
in from outer space, roaring in
my ears, "America! America!"

Mary Antin, "The Promised Land" (1912),
in *Autobiographies of American Jews,*
ed. Harold U. Ribalow (Philadelphia, 1965)

He is an American who, leaving behind him all his ancient prejudices and manners, receives new ones from the new mode of life he has embraced.... Americans are the western pilgrims. They carry along with them the great mass of arts, sciences, vigor, and industry which began long ago in the east. They will finish the great circle.

Michel Guillaume Jean de Crèvecoeur,
Letters from an American Farmer (1782)

PASSENGERS
NOT ALLOWED
ON THE BRIDGE

In the beginning of every American family we find people who had a clear view of themselves and their hopes. They were the immigrants. We are their sons daughters, and we have been witness to a miracle. Somehow the mixtures of heredity, opportunity, and individual desire came together and fashioned a great nation. We have realized the immigrant dream that here they would stake their futures so that their children would have a better life. It is an American idea—and it is working.

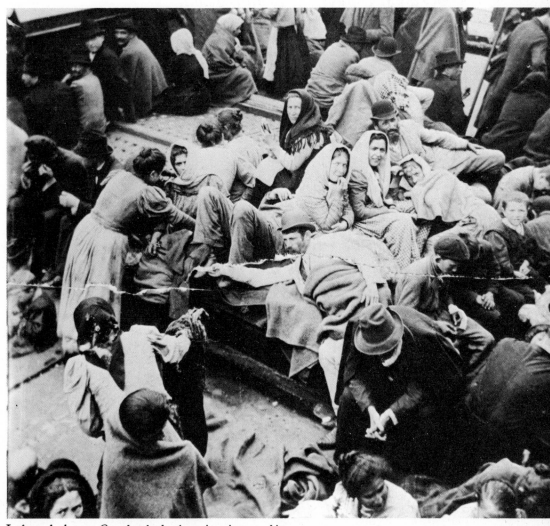

Left and above: *On the deck of an immigrant ship*

They came in waves for the same reasons that had always lured the immigrant—the twin hopes of prosperity and freedom. And they came steerage class, unable to afford the extra seven dollars and fifty cents per person for a cabin.

To Ellis Island went all the steerage passengers, frightened to death that they would forget the stories carefully contrived to get them past the famous twenty-two questions each person must answer. Every member of the family underwent a physical examination, and failure meant return. It was here that husbands and wives and children could be sent to the stairway of separation—the stairs leading to the "Holding Room" and exile from America.

When they had run the gauntlet of registration questions and medical inspection, they were ready. Only now, perhaps, did they begin to think about what awaited them— perhaps a relative, a railway ticket, or simply the golden streets of New York City.

The first home for hundreds of thousands of immigrants was the Lower East Side of New York. In every crowded, dingy apartment

there was always extra room for newcomers—not one to a room, but eight or ten undergoing the sudden transition to America.

There was a name for the new immigrant, so filled with derision that no one wanted it applied. It was "greenhorn." "Don't be a greenhorn," they said, "be American." And that meant getting American clothes, and getting them at a price.

On the Lower East Side it was the Irish immigrants who first occupied the houses. As they prospered, the Irish left the tenements to the Italians, the Jews, the Poles, and Russians that followed. In Harry Golden's words, the Irish became heroes, because after all, they had left the Lower East Side. They had, in ghetto terms, "gotten fat." As each succeeding generation of immigrants arrives, it looks with awe and admiration at those who have come just before. They all have left their mark.

I can't live with the old
world and am yet too green
for the new. I don't belong to
those with whom I was
educated. I am one of the
millions of immigrant
children, children of
loneliness, wandering
between two worlds that are
at once too old and too
new to live in.

Anzia Yezierska, *Children of Loneliness* (New York, 1923)

IN OUR FLAT we did not think of such a thing as storing the coal in the bathtub. There was no bathtub. So in the evening of the first day my father conducted us to the public baths. As we moved along in a little procession, I was delighted with the illumination of the streets. So many lamps, and they burned until morning, my father said, and so people did not need to carry lanterns. In America, then, everything was free, as we had heard in Russia. Light was free; the streets were as bright as a synagogue on a holy day. Music was free; we had been serenaded, to our gaping delight, by a brass band of many pieces soon after our installation on Union Place.

Education was free. That subject my father had written about repeatedly, as comprising his chief hope for us children, the essence of American opportunity, the treasure that no thief could touch, not even misfortune or poverty. It was the one thing that he was able to promise us when he sent for us; surer, safer than bread or shelter. On our second day, I was thrilled with the realization of what this freedom of education meant. A little girl from across the alley came and offered to conduct us to school. My father was out, but we five between us had a few words of English by this time. We knew the word school. We understood. This child, who had never seen us till yesterday, who could not pronounce our names, who was not much better dressed than we, was able to offer us the freedom of the schools of Boston! No application made, no questions asked, no examinations, rulings, exclusions; no machinations, no fees. The doors stood open for every one of us. The smallest child could show us the way.

Mary Antin, "The Promised Land," in *Autobiographies of American Jews,* ed. Harold U. Ribalow (Philadelphia, 1965)

MY FATHER came to this country from the little Russian town called Bialystok sixty-eight years ago. There was nothing in Russia for him. He had just served his term as a soldier. My mother was introduced to him and she married him, and a month later he left for the United States. She stayed on with her parents in this little Polish town, and my brother was born ten months later. Then my father sent for my mother. My brother was two and a half years old. They rented a room on the fifth floor, and they had to put a quarter into the meter for gas to heat up his milk. My father worked in the garment industry. At that time it was sweat shops, sixteen hours a day, and it was very, very hard. There was work, there wasn't work. My mother decided that, well, if we had to eat she had to do something, so she went out and did washing for other people. She put my brother into a nursery school and she would go to work, washing for other people and cleaning for other people. . . . My oldest brother at the age of six and a half was selling newspapers. When I was born, she got this tenement to be a janitor, because it was very hard to pay the rent. And she had these three holes. I mean they were dark, dreary places. We even had a boarder who paid us fifty cents a week. You put up a cot in the kitchen and this was it. . . . There was plenty of bedding, I remember. I remember my mother plucking the chickens and using it for feathers for the cushions. And she'd get the ticking and she'd make up her own pillows. And did the same with the bedding. I remember my mother as an old woman, all the time. She was thirty-eight when I was born. To me she looked like an old lady all her life.

Mamie Epstein
New York, N.Y.
February, 1973

Hudson State, New York
July 6th, 1828

Dear Parents,

I now sit me down to write to you, to let you know that we are all safe arrived in America, and are all much better than we have been; thank a merciful God for it. I often look back upon the scenes that we have passed through. While we were passing over the water our sufferings were great; but that God that is loving to all them that trust in him has brought us through. I will not grieve your hearts with all our sufferings, for my paper will not hold it. Little Mary was very ill with the fever that so many died with—7 children and one woman; to hear their cries and moans, it was very bad. I was so ill myself, that I was forced to crawl out of my bed, and lay on the floor while John made the bed. If you know of any coming here, tell them never to come where the vessel is so full; for we was shut down in darkness for a fortnight, till so many died; then the hatch was opened. I will not grieve your poor hearts with more about what we poor creatures suffered. . . .

We are in a land of plenty, and above all, where we can hear the sound of the Gospel. The gentleman that we work for, has preaching in his own parlours, till he can build a chapel; it has begun not a quarter of a mile from where we live: and many poor sinners be brought to Christ; for here is many that are drinking in of sin, like ox the water. And now, my dear sister, I must say something to thee. I hope these few lines will find you all well as we are at present; thank God for it. William told us to be sure to let him know how it was here; and if we liked the place he would come; so you must let him know all about it; and if he liked to come, no fear but what he will do well; but I know you cannot let him come

172

without you. I want you all here if you could go through the hardships of coming over. . . . [Give our] love to Elizabeth, and tell her if she wants fine clothes, she is to come here; it would be the making of her.

J. and E. Thorpe, "A Letter to the Parents in England," in *America's Immigrants,* ed. Rhoda Hoff (New York, 1967)

WE WOULD spend most of our vacation days in the streets, munching Indian nuts, or roasted peanuts, or hot chestnuts from the Italian at the corner . . . the whistling of his charcoal stove attracting our appetite. Or walking through the ghetto markets we would partake of hot lima beans, well baked; and brown or sweet potatoes straight from the oven; sour pickles, pickled watermelon, and most pleasurably, corn on the cob.

We were a Coxie's army as we swooped down upon the poor peddlers, arm in arm with our gang. . . .

We played potsy; went fishing for pennies, combs, and odd pieces of metal through street-corner grates; played jacks and marbles in the streets. A much-abused janitor would shoo the children from in front of his building with the words, "Come on, get out of here, quick, twenty-three skidoo."

Then we would follow the organ grinder with the monkey and buy some polly seeds and get a fortune for one cent, or we would watch the younger children dancing behind a hand-organ.

On rainy days we amused ourselves by writing our names backwards and holding the paper up to the mirror, to read forward; or hum a song through tissue paper on a comb, or by crossing out names of boys and girls against our own to see if the letters remaining which were dissimilar would spell the words "I love you."

We used to tap melodies in the manner of telegraphy, on the window, using our fingers as drum sticks, keeping each beat exactly so, and then wonder if anyone would recognize the tune by the shortness and the slowness of each tap. We made scrapbooks of important women or writers, of the day; of actors; of good pictures; of patriotic poems.

We played basketball in the yard of the school during the summer months and in the night school centers throughout the city; each week in a different center. We went to everything that was offered free. The concerts in the Mall in Central Park, where we heard Fritz Kreisler playing the violin. We experienced that chokey feeling in our throats, to hear such heavenly music. We went to Central Park, to see the animals or to go rowing. Or to Prospect Park, to picnic. We went on hikes, and it was nothing out of the ordinary to take a short walk, say from 14th Street to 110th Street. We greatly appreciated the crowds in the streets; we did not feel lonely one bit. We enjoyed seeing a parade on Fifth Avenue as though it were a Grand Opera performance. . . .

Mother was having a baby in an East Broadway maternity hospital. So I became the cook. Also, standing on a box, I scrubbed the children's overalls and stockings. My dad was experiencing one of his idle periods.

He sat at his sewing machine, thinking of his father in the Old Country; he, too, had sat at just such a sewing machine; and what did he make? Petticoats! So be it! If it was good enough for his father, it would be good enough for him! He took his last few dollars that he had saved to get mother out of the hospital, and bought some white calico and yards of white lace and began to make some petticoats. Perhaps he could sell them quickly before mother came home from the hospital; but who could sell them on a pushcart for him?

"Growing Up on New York's Lower East Side, by a Young Polish Girl (Early 1900's)," in *America's Immigrants,* ed. Rhoda Hoff (New York, 1967)

SOON the entire neighborhood in which I lived became a school room, so to speak. As I walked in the streets I would pronounce aloud the words I saw written on signs, on billboards, or street corners. "Butcher shop," I slowly spelled out. "Gayety Burlesque" (what a strange word!), "Shoes Repaired Here," "Uneeda Biscuit." Mumbling to myself, I would stand before some store window struggling with a strange, unintelligible word until an irate shopkeeper told me to move on. I did move on but only to take up my post at another establishment, for I was determined to learn to speak my adopted language fluently even if the entire East Side had to listen painfully to my lessons.

One of the first things I learned was that if I were ultimately to study law I would first have to find a job. In the house in which I lived everyone worked, men, women, and even children, and before long I joined their ranks.

Getting a job in those days had a certain directness about it which is lacking in our larger American cities today. My sisters told me where the various factories were located, and all I had to do was to go from door to door to find out whether anyone could use my services.

Finally I stumbled across a chandelier

factory on Canal Street which proclaimed on a crudely painted sign—but in three languages—that a "hand" was wanted inside. I walked up several flights of stairs and finally spoke to the foreman. He looked me over, and made careful note of my husky appearance, and told me I could start working. My salary was to be two dollars a week.

Louis Waldman, *Labor Lawyer* (New York, 1944)

EVERY STREET had a "Cheap Charlie." I used to wonder at the singularity of the candy-store business being exclusively in the hands of men of the same name. These candy stores had an extraordinary attraction for children because of the personal attitude of Charlie to his young customers. This was an even more potent lure than the advertised cheapness of Charlie's wares, which we accepted on faith without inquiry or comparison. Charlie was human and understanding, and was not above entering into the problems of his patrons. Thus it was possible, when one did not happen to have a penny at the moment, to confide in Charlie and, on a promise to pay up at the first opportunity, to leave the store with the chocolate-covered walnuts in a paper bag.

The groceryman was less understanding. I suspected that my mother was responsible for his insistence on prompt payment for "broken cake." Nor did I have the heart to blame her. Her own relations with the man were often delicate. I myself had witnessed humiliating scenes in which he categorically refused to give her further credit. But my mother always managed to persuade him to change his mind, alleging an imminent favorable turn of events for us which would promptly take care of all our financial indebtedness.

"Life on Stanton Street," in *Autobiographies of American Jews,* ed. Harold U. Ribalow (Philadelphia, 1965)

The school was established about fifteen years ago, and has grown with the Jewish population from one class of twenty-five pupils to twenty-two classes having about eleven hundred pupils ranging in age from six to fifteen years. There are no charges for instruction, and besides being a free school in all that the term implies, needy children who attend are supplied with shoes and clothing. The money for maintaining the institution comes from the annual dues of the members, of whom there are about two thousand, and from contributions from Russian Jews who wish to pay more than the stipulated $3 a year. There is probably no schoolhouse in New York in which less money has been expended for interior decoration than this Hebrew School.

New York Tribune
November 12, 1899

SMELLS, in general, played an important part in our lives. Not an unpleasant part, I recall, but one that in its way made life a little easier, serving for identification of persons, their habits and social position, perhaps as clues to character and occupation. Everything and everybody had a smell. Some smells were generic and impersonal, others particular, like the leitmotifs in the music dramas of Richard Wagner. And just as the introduction of a leitmotif warns the listener that the personage it represents is about to appear, so the insinuation of a smell in a room usually heralded the approach of the person who had become identified with it. Immigrants, however, could not so be identified individually for at least a year or two after their arrival, as their own odors were overpowered by and absorbed into the more exigent smell of "ship."

Old people had, in general, an acrid smell, and old men invariably smelled of snuff. Young people and children merely smelled unwashed. We knew that we too would smell of snuff when we grew old. That was in the nature of things. Life was stern and realistic, and the conditions it imposed were not subject to question or criticism. After taking snuff it was quite proper for people to blow their noses without the interposition of a handkerchief. In rooms not graced with spittoons, what was more natural than to spit on the floor! It was natural, though not desirable, for children to have lice in their hair and for grown-ups to harbor them in the seams of their clothing and underwear. Beds and bedding and all overstuffed furniture were infested with bedbugs. The pests were periodically hunted and exterminated; but their presence was not considered a disgrace, and they shared with poverty and disease the status of divine visitation. "What brand of bedbug powder do you use?" was a natural query when housewives met on the street. . . . The world was most probably the same for everybody.

We knew that rich people had more rooms, better food and clothing, and easier lives than the poor; but we had no reason to believe that their lot was otherwise different, or that they were exempt from what we believed to be universal afflictions. On the visible world, half of which we knew first-hand, and the other half of which we could only imagine, there were, for us, certain unchangeable phenomena: children were dirty and were obliged to scratch their heads; mothers were unkempt and slatternly; everybody, old and young, had teeth pulled regularly, so that middle-aged and old people had few if any teeth; a great many children died young; everybody slept in underwear; parents always quarreled; mothers were generally indulgent to their children, but fathers either kept aloof or were brutal to them.

And, of course, everyone over fourteen years of age was employed in gainful labor. Not before the age of fourteen could one obtain one's working papers. It took a a considerable amount of experience in the realm of what is now called "the underprivileged" before I could collate these observations, draw my conclusions, and, by extension, relate the picture thus built up to that part of the world which lay outside my knowledge and beyond my reach.

"Life on Stanton Street,"
in *Autobiographies of American Jews,*
ed. Harold U. Ribalow (Philadelphia, 1965)

The immigrant and his descendants left something of themselves, imprints great or small, which can be seen if we care to look. The carvings and designs are the poignant legacy of unknown stonecutters and woodcarvers, and perhaps these are the truly great monuments.

The aging skeletons of liberty are the wars and crises that afflict a nation. But the substance of history is found in dusty articles and treasured scrapbooks. The names are Cartwright, Koslovsky, Schultz, and Chavez. We do not know their dreams or achievements, but in their expressions is the mark of a new spirit.

My father and mother came steerage class from Russia. Cabin class passengers didn't have to go to Ellis Island, but my parents did, worried sick that something would go wrong and they'd be sent away.

My father remembered having a name tag pinned to his clothes that he couldn't read. He spent four days on Ellis Island and considered himself lucky, because some people were there for two months waiting for clearance. There was always a frightening rumor passed in a dozen languages that something had gone wrong, that none of them would be allowed to enter.

My parents really believed that in America they would find gold bricks in the streets. It didn't take long for them to realize that what they discovered was far more valuable. Here they had the right to dream of a better life for their children. That was their gift to me —to all of us—and perhaps it's the source of this country's strength. I've tried often to tell the story to my four sons, because I think it's worth retelling.

Kirk Douglas

In their native country, education was an expensive luxury reserved for the aristocracy. In America it was free. Education—the magic golden world of education. Nowhere are the hopes of the immigrant so clearly crystallized as in the drive to have their children go to school.

It was the key to tomorrow that they had promised themselves when they arrived. No matter what else —how poor, how hard a life—in the children was invested the dream, and come hell or high water, they would accomplish it.

I always looked forward to living in a better place because I would visit my cousins living in the Bronx and Brooklyn. They always had the bathroom in the house and no bathroom out in the hallway. We had the bathtub in the kitchen and a little porcelain sink to wash in every morning. That's just what we would use. And when I would go visit my cousins in Brownsville, it was a beautiful place to live, and when I visited my cousins in the Bronx, they all lived in beautiful houses. To me it was beautiful. They had rooms that were nice and clean and wide and they had privacy. Our rooms weren't private. They were just rooms that were separated by a couple of boards—by walls that didn't mean anything. There was no closet space. You had maybe one little tiny closet. And everything else hung on walls covered with clothing.

Mamie Epstein
New York, N.Y.
February, 1973

He said he just wanted me to learn a trade. He said that later on, if you have nothing else to do, that you could always fall back to your trade. I guess I never left. I got to like it, and my brother and I, now that my father has passed on, we have a nice business and people are wonderful. They're nice, I guess, because of the warmth of the Italian people here in Little Italy. Now there's a little change in people. I guess their children are getting married and they've moved out of this section, but usually they make a visit once in a while.

Dominic Desanti
New York, N.Y.
February, 1973

Italian clam seller on Mulberry Street, New York City

I WAS now on my way across the world to America. I was young, I was hopeful, and for the first time in my life I had seventy-five dollars in ready cash in my pocket. My tickets were paid for in advance, my practical father having made all the arrangements through a travel agent. . . .

I traveled steerage to America—and I marvel at the equanimity with which I write these words. Crossing the Atlantic in steerage was a terrifying and nauseating experience. There were some forty or fifty men, women, and children crowded into one room with absolutely no ventilation other than that provided by the hatchway through which we had entered. Cots were set up in tiers with just enough space between the sets of bunks for one person to squeeze through with difficulty. The odors were indescribable, and breathing was far from a reflex activity; it required actual effort. Baggage had to be kept either on the floor or beneath the cot itself. People were constantly stumbling over stray bags and packages.

We ate at long tables and from large bowls into which the entire meal, except for liquids, was dumped. But the foul odors of the ship and of unwashed bodies packed into close quarters were not conducive to hearty eating. In a way this was fortunate, because there was not enough food for all. It was only after seasickness began to take its toll that those who could eat had enough food. After starving my way across Europe, at first I attacked the ship's victuals ravenously. But I could not stomach them for long and spent the rest of the trip detesting food and longing for an end to this tormenting journey.

Wasted, unsteady on my feet, but still hopeful, I arrived at Battery Park, New York, on September 17, 1909. Behind me was the bustling harbor with its innumerable boats, the sight of which made me seasick all over again. Facing me, beyond the open spaces of the park, were the tall buildings of lower Manhattan, buildings which were more magnificent and higher than any I had ever imagined, even in my wildest dreams of this metropolis of the New World.

No one had come to meet me, for no one knew precisely when I was to arrive. And there I stood in Battery Park in my tight pants and round hat, with my knowledge of the Talmud, Yiddish, and Ukrainian, but in abysmal ignorance of English. I wandered around the park for some time, trying to find someone who could understand my language and direct me to 118 Orchard Street, where my sister Cecilia lived. After enduring the blank stares of several park bench idlers I at last discovered someone who understood me, and I was off via horse-car in the direction of the Lower East Side.

When I got to the Orchard Street address I had to climb five flights of rickety and malodorous stairs to my sister's tenement flat. It was the first day of Rosh Hashanah and all my four sisters were there, seated around a festive table. They were at the same time overjoyed and alarmed when I walked in, for I was pale and gaunt from hunger and from the days I had spent below decks. They had known, of course, that I was coming, but my difficulties with the fraudulent travel agent and the delay in Rotterdam had confused them as to the exact day and hour of my arrival.

First on the order of business for the new immigrant was a visit to a clothing store.

"You think you can walk around like that, looking as green as grass?" my sister Anna said. "Why, no one, not even a peddler, will give you a job!"

And so it was that I parted forever with my tight pants, my round hat, and my high, creaking Ukrainian boots.

My American store clothes became a sort of passport which gave me the right to walk the streets as an equal of anyone and to consider myself as belonging to this vast city. This cheap, ready-to-wear East Side suit bridged the first gap, a sartorial gap, to be sure, between my past and my present.

Louis Waldman,
Labor Lawyer (New York, 1944)

WE WENT one day to Newark and got work on the street. We paid a man five dollars each for getting us the work, and we were with that boss for six months. He was Irish, but a good man, and he gave us our money every Saturday night. When the work was done we each had nearly two hundred dollars saved. Plenty of the men spoke English and they taught us, and we taught them to read and write. That was at night, for we had a lamp in our room, and there were only five other men who lived in that room with us.

We got up at half-past five o'clock every morning, and made coffee on the stove and had a breakfast of bread and cheese, onions, garlick, and red herrings. We went to work at seven o'clock and in the middle of the day we had soup and bread in a place where we got it for two cents a plate.

Rocco Corresca, "A Boy Immigrant from Italy (Early 1900s)," in *America's Immigrants*, ed. Rhoda Hoff (New York, 1967)

THE ONE THING completely lacking in my boyhood was play, at least play in the ordinary sense of carefree, undirected activities with children of my own age. When I was very small I undoubtedly had toys, but I cannot remember any specific objects that might have beguiled my days in Illinois, and after I arrived in California I know that there were no playthings. Not only had we no money for such luxuries, but life was far too grim a reality to have allowed for even the slight detachment needed for the establishment of a mood of play. The older children did not play; they all had serious tasks to perform. Following their example, I did not play either, and it was not long before I had other completely occupying things to do.

"Boyhood in San Francisco,"
in *Autobiographies of American Jews,*
ed. Harold U. Ribalow (Philadelphia, 1965)

The canals and railroads built largely by the Irish immigrants of the 1840s and '50s are almost relics of the past, and the mines that lured the Poles and Serbs and Germans are often deserted skeletons, but the spirit remains a tangible bequest of our forebears.

The man who has no money will do best if he begins by hiring himself out to a farmer as an extra hand. In six months he should easily be able to put aside the sum of fifty dollars, out of which he can buy himself forty acres of Congress-land—meaning land which has not as yet been brought under cultivation.

He will, of course, have to exert himself mightily to make his land fruitful the first year, if he begins in the spring; but if once he manages to get through that first year, he need never worry again about feeding himself. And in the course of the next three or four years, he should already be in a position to exchange a portion of his harvest for money or provisions at the markets which are to be found everywhere. . . .

The immigrant, especially the man who has no money, must be self-reliant and he cannot be lacking in endurance. Whoever is fainthearted and incapable of standing on his own feet under any conditions that life may confront him with, had better not come over here.

E. H. Thomson,
The Emigrant's Guide to the State of Michigan (1849)

I would advise no one who is in a steady way of business at home, however small, and who can make both ends meet by strict economy, to think of emigrating. It is a sore trial, and if I had been a single man, with no one to provide for but myself, I would never have left Scotland. I often think now that a bite in that country would do me more good than a bellyful in this. The man that comes here only exchanges evils: he is obliged to mingle with a most profane and godless set, he cannot give his children a religious education, and it is shocking to think of the depravity they must witness from their infancy: compared with this, I am not sure that poverty is not the least evil.

A Scottish captain (1833), in *America's Immigrants,* ed. Rhoda Hoff (New York, 1967)

JESUS MENDIZABEL: I was born in Zacatecas [Mexico] . . . In those days no matter how much one worked one hardly earned a *real,* scarcely enough for food. So when some friends told me that one could earn good money here in the United States I managed to come by way of El Paso as far as Phoenix. . . . It isn't the same here as in Mexico, where one has to work with nothing but one's muscle, in the mud with everything dirty. Here the mines are clean and a lot of machinery is used, so that one doesn't have to exert one's self very much. What more could I have wished? I was earning more, had a sure job, and didn't work very hard. So I kept on until now I have grown old. When I came here [to Phoenix] . . . this looked like a farm. Now it is a large city. . . . I have been in hotels, I have worked cleaning the city streets, as a laborer in business houses, and altogether in a great many things. The important thing to me was to earn my living honestly. . . . I have three children now; they are . . . all going to school. . . . I pray to God that He may give me life to go on working, for I would rather die than take them out of school. I want them to amount to something, to learn all they can, since I didn't learn anything.

Manuel Gamio,
The Mexican Immigrant (New York, 1969)

THE community lived toughly by its own code. Chinese ethics could not be honored by Western courts; they were implemented either peacefully or violently by Chinese organizations. Enterprises such as caring for the sick or providing burials for the dead were duties of "Benevolent Associations," whose members spoke a common dialect based on their various geographical Cantonese origins. Protection of property rights or from persecution was assumed by membership in a family name clan of greater power (such as all the Chans in their clan, and all the Wongs in theirs). . . .

It was the ambition of most of the men to work and save in the United States and return to China . . . But my father . . . attending night classes at the Methodist Chinese Mission in San Francisco to learn English, was exposed to Christian theory and the practical kindness of Christian Westerners. The Golden Rule did not conflict with the Confucian doctrines . . . The measure of human dignity accorded to Western women particularly impressed him. . . . My father wrote to his family, "In America, I have learned how shamefully women in China have been treated. I will bleach the disgrace of my ancestors by bringing my wife and two daughters to San Francisco, where my wife can work without disgrace and my daughters shall have the opportunity of education." . . .

To support the family in America, Daddy . . . finally settled on manufacturing men's and children's denim garments. He leased sewing equipment, installed machines in a basement where rent was cheapest, and there he and his family lived and worked. There was no thought that dim and airless quarters were terrible conditions for living and working, or that child labor was unhealthful. The only goal was for all in the family to work, to save, to become educated. It was possible, so it would be done. . . .

My eldest brother . . . was cherished in the best Chinese tradition. He had his own room; he kept a German Shepherd as his pet; he was tutored by a Chinese scholar; he was sent to private school for American classes. As a male Wong, he would be responsible some day for the preservation of and pilgrimages to ancestral graves—his privileges were his birthright. We girls were content with the unusual opportunities of working and attending two schools. . . . By day, I attended American public school. From 5:00 p.m. to 8:00 p.m. on five weekdays and from 9:00 a.m. to 12 noon on Saturdays, I attended the Chinese school. . . . We studied by exacting memorization. . . . There was little time for play, and toys were unknown to me. In any spare time, I was supplied with embroidery and sewing for my mother. . . .

We were molded to be trouble-free, unobtrusive, quiescent, cooperative. . . . Daughters were all expected to be of one standard. To allow each one of many daughters to be different would have posed enormous problems of cost, energy, and attention. No one was shown physical affection. Such familiarity would have weakened my parents and endangered the one-answer authoritative system. One standard from past to present, whether in China or in San Francisco, was simpler to enforce. Still, am I not lucky that I am alive to tell this story?

Jade Snow Wong, "Puritans from the Orient," in *The Immigrant Experience,* ed. Thomas C. Wheeler (New York, 1971)

There is no country in the world where it is conceivable that a man of my origins could be standing here next to the President of the United States. And if my origin can contribute anything to the formulation of our policies, it is that at an early age I have seen what can happen to a society that is based on hatred and strength and distrust, and that I experienced then what America means to other people—its hope and its idealism.

Henry Kissinger
Washington, D.C.
September 22, 1973

Rediscovery

By working with the soil which
doesn't lie to you and by working
with the wood which doesn't lie to
you, and having to tackle problems
which are really basic, you learn
a kind of honesty and a realism
that is really strong. You know,
you can just feel it in the roots of
all the farmers throughout history.

Student at University of California,
Santa Cruz

The legacy remains of the romance with the land, the pride of ownership, the energy to work, the passion to expand, and the satisfaction of taking from it the sustenance of life.

This experience of rediscovering what might be called tradition of values is really the rediscovery of that bond, the earth. It's not discovering something that's old-fashioned; it's something that's completely new and revitalizing. And that's one of the feelings that makes me want to sustain this experience for myself and for other people.

Student at University of California, Santa Cruz

"Those who labor in the earth are the chosen people of God," *Thomas Jefferson wrote. As an experiment in pioneer living, students at the University of California at Santa Cruz have started a farm on seventeen acres of virgin land, using methods and tools that date back two hundred years.*

We grow our own food, we make our own clothes, we build our own buildings. We experience these things directly—I guess it gets back to the spiritual thing.

Student at University of California, Santa Cruz

This is America,
This vast, confused beauty,
This staring, restless speed of
  loveliness,
Mighty, overwhelming, crude, of
  all forms,
Making grandeur out of profusion,
Afraid of no incongruities,
Sublime in its audacity,
Bizarre breaker of moulds.

Amy Lowell, "The Congressional Liberty,"
Complete Poetical Works (Boston, 1955)

The map of America goes on and
on. The map of America is a map of
endlessness, of opening out, of forever and ever. No man's face
would make you think of it but his
hope might, his courage might.

Archibald MacLeish

When an American says that he
loves his country, he means not
only that he loves the New England
hills, the prairies glistening in the
sun, the wide and rising plains, the
great mountains, and the sea. He
means that he loves an inner air,
an inner light in which freedom
lives and in which a man can
draw the breath of self-respect.

Adlai Stevenson
New York, N.Y.
August 27, 1952

For this is what America is all about. It is the uncrossed desert and the unclimbed ridge. It is the harvest that is sleeping in the unplowed ground.

Lyndon B. Johnson, *This America* (New York, 1966)

Plowing with a horse team at the Santa Cruz experimental farm

Below: *Working in the fields at the Santa Cruz student farm*
Following pages: *The University of California experimental farm at Santa Cruz: carrying stakes for the fields* (top) *and the cabbage patch* (bottom)

America
How They Saw It

One country, one constitution, one destiny.

Daniel Webster, Speech, March 15, 1837

Yesterday the greatest
question was decided which
ever was debated in America;
and a greater perhaps never
was, nor will be, decided
among men. A resolution was
passed without one dissenting
colony, that these United
Colonies are, and of right
ought to be, free and
independent States.

John Adams
Letter to Abigail Adams
July 3, 1776

An enlightened Englishman when he first
lands on this continent . . . says to himself,
this is the work of my countrymen, who,
when convulsed by factions, afflicted by a
variety of miseries and wants, restless and
impatient, took refuge here. They brought
along with them their national genius, to
which they principally owe what liberty
they enjoy, and what substance they possess.
Here he sees the industry of his native country displayed in a new manner, and traces
in their works the embryos of all the arts,
sciences, and ingenuity which flourish in
Europe. Here he beholds fair cities, substantial villages, extensive fields, an immense
country filled with decent houses, good
roads, orchards, meadows, and bridges,
where a hundred years ago all was wild,
woody, and uncultivated!

Michel Guillaume Jean de Crèvecoeur,
Letters from an American Farmer (1782)

America is a hell of a success.

Joseph Gurney "Uncle Joe" Cannon

What then is the American, this new man? He is either an European, or the descendant of an European, hence that strange mixture of blood, which you will find in no other country. I could point out to you a family whose grandfather was an Englishman, whose wife was Dutch, whose son married a French woman, and whose present four sons have now four wives of different nations. *He* is an American, who, leaving behind him all his ancient prejudices and manners, receives new ones from the new mode of life he has embraced, the new government he obeys, and the new rank he holds. He becomes an American by being received in the broad lap of our great *Alma Mater*. Here individuals of all nations are melted into a new race of man, whose labors and posterity will one day cause great changes in the world. Americans are the western pilgrims, who are carrying along with them that great mass of arts, sciences, vigor, and industry which began long since in the east; they will finish the great circle. . . . The American is a new man, who acts upon new principles; he must therefore entertain new ideas, and form new opinions. From involuntary idleness, servile dependence, penury, and useless labor, he has passed to toils of a very different nature, rewarded by ample subsistence.—This is an American.

Michel Guillaume Jean de Crèvecoeur,
Letters from an American Farmer (1782)

The United States themselves
are essentially the greatest
poem. . . . Here at last is
something in the doings of
man that corresponds with the
broadcast doings of the day
and night.

Walt Whitman,
Preface to *Leaves of Grass* (1855)

If the picturesque were
banished from the face of the
earth, I think the idea would
survive in some typical
American breast.

Henry James,
Transatlantic Sketches (1875)

A truly American sentiment
recognizes the dignity of labor
and the fact that honor lies in
honest toil.

Grover Cleveland
Letter accepting nomination for the Presidency
August 18, 1884

Of "Americanism" of the right
sort we cannot have too much.
Mere vaporing and boasting
become a nation as little as a
man. But honest, outspoken
pride and faith in our country
are infinitely better and more
to be respected than the
cultivated reserve which sets
it down as ill-bred and in bad
taste ever to refer to our
country except by way of
deprecation, criticism, or
general negation.

Henry Cabot Lodge
Address, New England Society of New York
December 22, 1884

It was in making education not
only common to all, but in some
sense compulsory on all, that
the destiny of the free republics
of America was practically
settled.

James Russell Lowell,
"New England Two Centuries Ago"

Together they gave to the nation and the world undying proof that Americans of African descent possess the pride, courage, and devotion of the patriot soldier. One hundred and eight thousand such Americans enlisted under the Union flag in 1863–1865.

Charles William Eliot
Inscription on Robert Gould Shaw Monument,
Boston Common (1897)

Little of beauty has America given the world save the rude grandeur God himself stamped on her bosom; the human spirit in this new world has expressed itself in vigor and ingenuity rather than in beauty.

W. E. B. Du Bois,
The Souls of Black Folk (1903)

There is one day that is ours. There is one day when all we Americans who are not self-made go back to the old home to eat saleratus biscuits and marvel how much nearer to the porch the old pump looks than it used to. . . . Thanksgiving Day . . . is the one day that is purely American.

O. Henry (William Sydney Porter), "Two Thanksgiving Day Gentlemen," in *The Trimmed Lamp* (1907)

The things that the flag stands for were created by the experiences of a great people. Everything that it stands for was written by their lives. The flag is the embodiment, not of sentiment, but of history. It represents the experiences made by men and women, the experiences of those who do and live under that flag.

Woodrow Wilson Address June 14, 1915

There is no room in this
country for hyphenated
Americanism. . . . The one
absolutely certain way of
bringing this nation to ruin, of
preventing all possibility of its
continuing to be a nation at all,
would be to permit it to
become a tangle of squabbling
nationalities.

Theodore Roosevelt
Speech before the Knights of Columbus
New York, N.Y., October 12, 1915

Sometimes people call me an
idealist. Well, that is the way
I know I am an American.
America is the only idealistic
nation in the world.

Woodrow Wilson
Address in Sioux Falls, So. Dakota
September 8, 1919

I believe in the United States of
America as a Government of the
people, by the people, for the people;
whose just powers are derived from
the consent of the governed; a de-
mocracy in a republic, a sovereign
Nation of many sovereign States;
a perfect Union one and insepar-
able, established upon those principles of freedom, equality, justice
and humanity for which American
patriots sacrificed their lives and
fortunes. I therefore believe it is my
duty to my country to love it, to support its Constitution, to obey its
laws, to respect its flag, and to
defend it against all enemies.

William Tyler Page,
"The American's Creed" (1918)

America is the place where you cannot kill your government by killing the men who conduct it.

Woodrow Wilson
Address in Helena, Montana
September 11, 1919

In the United States there is more space where nobody is than where anybody is. This is what makes America what it is.

Gertrude Stein,
The Geographical History of America (1936)

It is a great number of people
on pilgrimage, common and
ordinary people, charged with
the usual human failings, yet
filled with such a hope as
never caught the imaginations
and the hearts of any nation
on earth before. The hope of
liberty. The hope of justice.
The hope of a land in which a
man can stand straight,
without fear, without rancor.

R. L. Duffus
Editorial in the *New York Times* (June 14, 1940)

The primary concern of
American education today is
not the development of the
appreciation of the "good life"
in young gentlemen born to
the purple.... Our purpose is
to cultivate in the largest
possible number of our future
citizens an appreciation of both
the responsibilities and the
benefits which come to them
because they are Americans
and are free.

James Bryant Conant
Annual Report to the Board of Overseers,
Harvard University
January 11, 1943

America has never forgotten–
and will never forget–the
nobler things that brought her
into being and that light her
path–the path that was entered
upon only one hundred and
fifty years ago. . . . How young
she is! It will be centuries
before she will adopt that
maturity of custom–the
clothing of the grave–that
some people believe she is
already fitted for.

Bernard M. Baruch
Address on accepting The Churchman Award
New York, N.Y., May 23, 1944

When Kansas and Colorado
have a quarrel over the water
in the Arkansas River they
don't call out the National
Guard in each State and go to
war over it. They bring a suit
in the Supreme Court of the
United States and abide by the
decision. There isn't a reason
in the world why we cannot
do that internationally.

Harry S Truman
Speech in Kansas City, Kan.
April, 1945

God and the politicians willing, the United States can declare peace upon the world, and win it.

Ely Culbertson,
Must We Fight Russia? (1946)

America is a passionate idea or it is nothing. America is a human brotherhood or it is a chaos.

Max Lerner,
"The United States as Exclusive Hotel,"
in *Actions and Passions* (1949)

America is so vast that almost everything said about it is likely to be true, and the opposite is probably equally true.

James T. Farrell,
Introduction to H. L. Mencken's *Prejudices: A Selection* (1958)

The American, by nature, is optimistic. He is experimental, an inventor and a builder who builds best when called upon to build greatly.

John F. Kennedy
Address in Washington, D.C.
January 1, 1960

In America, with all its evils
and faults, you can still reach
through the forest and see
the sun.

> Dick Gregory,
> "One Less Door,"
> in *Nigger* (1964)

For we are a nation of
believers. Underneath the
clamor of building and the
rush of our day's pursuits, we
are believers in justice and
liberty and union. And in our
own Union we believe that
every man must some day be
free. And we believe in
ourselves.

> Lyndon B. Johnson,
> *This America*
> (New York, 1966)